Street by Street

DOVER, FOL
ASHFORD
DEAL, HYTHE, TENTERDEN

Bethersden, Brabourne Lees, Densole, Elham, Hamstreet, Hawkinge, Kennington, Kingsdown, Kingsnorth, Lyminge, St Michaels, Whitfield, Willesborough, Wye

1st edition March 2008
© Automobile Association Developments Limited 2008

 This product includes map data licensed from Ordnance Survey® with the permission of the Controller of Her Majesty's Stationery Office. © Crown copyright 2008. All rights reserved. Licence number 100021153.

The copyright in all PAF is owned by Royal Mail Group plc.

Published by AA Publishing (a trading name of Automobile Association Developments Limited, whose registered office is Fanum House, Basing View, Basingstoke, Hampshire RG21 4EA. Registered number 1878835).

Produced by the Mapping Services Department of The Automobile Association. (A03563)

A CIP Catalogue record for this book is available from the British Library.

Printed by Oriental Press in Dubai

Ref: ML274

Key to map pages	ii-iii
Key to map symbols	iv-1
Enlarged map pages	2-7
Main map pages	8-75
Index – towns & villages	76
Index – streets	77-83
Index – featured places	83-84
Acknowledgements	84

ii

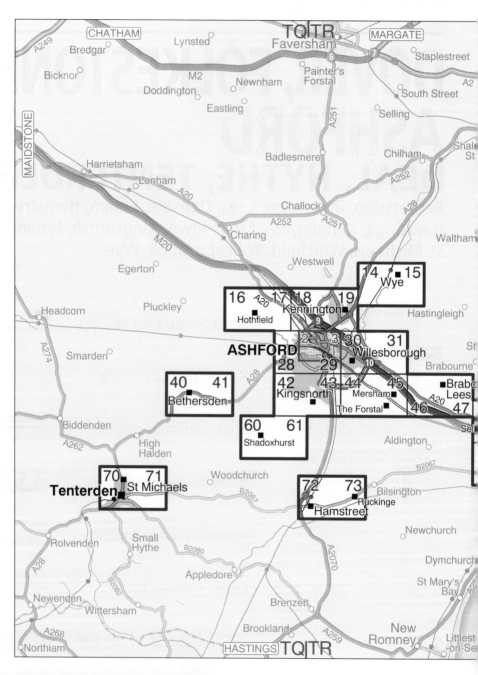

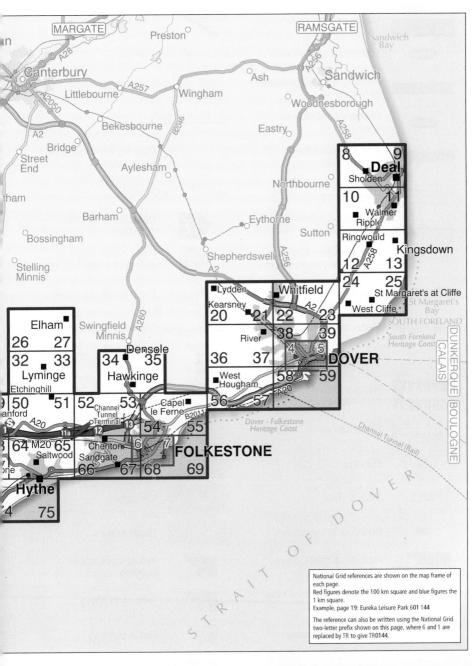

MARGATE   Preston   RAMSGATE   Sandwich Bay

Canterbury   Ash   Sandwich
Littlebourne   A257   Wingham
                                        Woodnesborough
Bekesbourne   Eastry
Bridge
Street End   Aylesham   Northbourne
                                                          8   Deal   9
tham   Sholden
          Barham   Eythorne   10   11
Bossingham   Sutton   Walmer
                                              Ripple
Stelling Minnis   Shepherdswell   Ringwould   Kingsdown
                    A2   12   13
                                              24   25
Elham   Swingfield Minnis   Lydden   Whitfield   St Margaret's at Cliffe
                              Kearsney   West Cliffe   St Margaret's Bay
26   27   20   21   22   23   SOUTH FORELAND
32   33   Densole   34   35   River   38   39   South Foreland Heritage Coast
Lyminge   Hawkinge   36   37   4   5   DOVER
Etchinghill   West Hougham   58   59
50   51   52   53   Capel le Ferne   56   57
anford   Channel Tunnel Terminal   54   55   Dover - Folkestone Heritage Coast   Channel Tunnel (Rail)
64 M20 65   13   6   7   FOLKESTONE
Saltwood   Cheriton Sandgate   66   67 68   69
Hythe
4   75

DUNKERQUE CALAIS   BOULOGNE

STRAIT OF DOVER

National Grid references are shown on the map frame of each page.
Red figures denote the 100 km square and blue figures the 1 km square.
Example, page 19: Eureka Leisure Park 601 144

The reference can also be written using the National Grid two-letter prefix shown on this page, where 6 and 1 are replaced by TR to give TR0144.

4.2 inches to 1 mile   **Scale of main map pages**   **1:15,000**

0   1/4   miles   1/2   3/4   1
0   1/4   1/2   kilometres 3/4   1   1 1/4   1 1/2

iv

Symbol	Description
Junction 9	Motorway & junction
Services	Motorway service area
	Primary road single/dual carriageway
Services	Primary road service area
	A road single/dual carriageway
	B road single/dual carriageway
	Other road single/dual carriageway
	Minor/private road, access may be restricted
← ←	One-way street
	Pedestrian area
	Track or footpath
	Road under construction
	Road tunnel
P	Parking
P+	Park & Ride
	Bus/coach station
	Railway & main railway station
	Railway & minor railway station
⊖	Underground station
⊖	Light railway & station
+++++++++	Preserved private railway

Symbol	Description
LC	Level crossing
•—•—•—•	Tramway
- - - - - -	Ferry route
....	Airport runway
— · — · — · —	County, administrative boundary
▼▼▼▼▼▼▼▼	Mounds
17	Page continuation 1:15,000
3	Page continuation to enlarged scale 1:10,000
	River/canal, lake, pier
	Aqueduct, lock, weir
465 ▲ Winter Hill	Peak (with height in metres)
	Beach
	Woodland
	Park
	Cemetery
	Built-up area
	Industrial/business building
	Leisure building
	Retail building
	Other building

⊓⊓⊓⊓⊓⊓	City wall	⚔	Castle
A&E	Hospital with 24-hour A&E department	🏛	Historic house or building
PO	Post Office	Wakehurst Place (NT)	National Trust property
📖	Public library	Ⓜ	Museum or art gallery
ℹ	Tourist Information Centre	♞	Roman antiquity
ℹ	Seasonal Tourist Information Centre	⚱	Ancient site, battlefield or monument
⛽⛽	Petrol station, 24 hour Major suppliers only	🏭	Industrial interest
✝	Church/chapel	❋	Garden
🚻	Public toilets	◉	Garden Centre Garden Centre Association Member
♿	Toilet with disabled facilities	🌱	Garden Centre Wyevale Garden Centre
PH	Public house AA recommended	🌳	Arboretum
🍴	Restaurant AA inspected	🐄	Farm or animal centre
Madeira Hotel	Hotel AA inspected	🦌	Zoological or wildlife collection
🎭	Theatre or performing arts centre	🐦	Bird collection
🎬	Cinema	🦆	Nature reserve
⚑	Golf course	🐟	Aquarium
▲	Camping AA inspected	V	Visitor or heritage centre
🚐	Caravan site AA inspected	♈	Country park
▲🚐	Camping & caravan site AA inspected	◔	Cave
🎢	Theme park	🌾	Windmill
⛪	Abbey, cathedral or priory	🛢	Distillery, brewery or vineyard

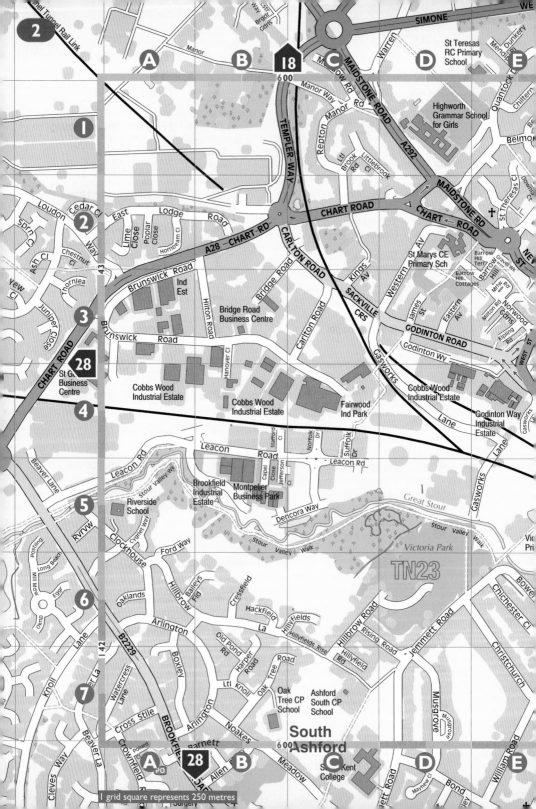

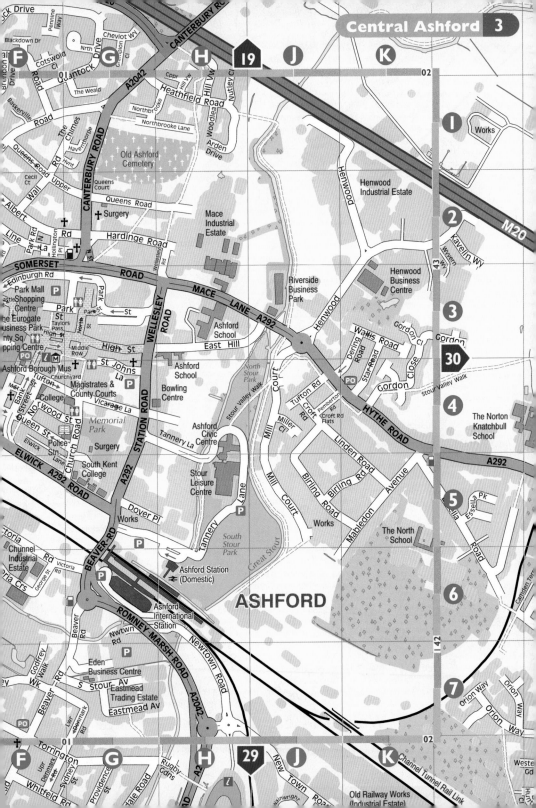

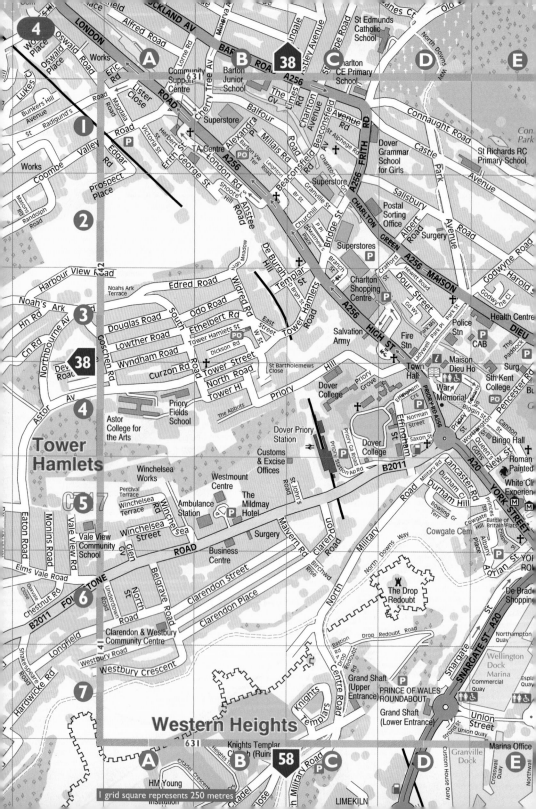

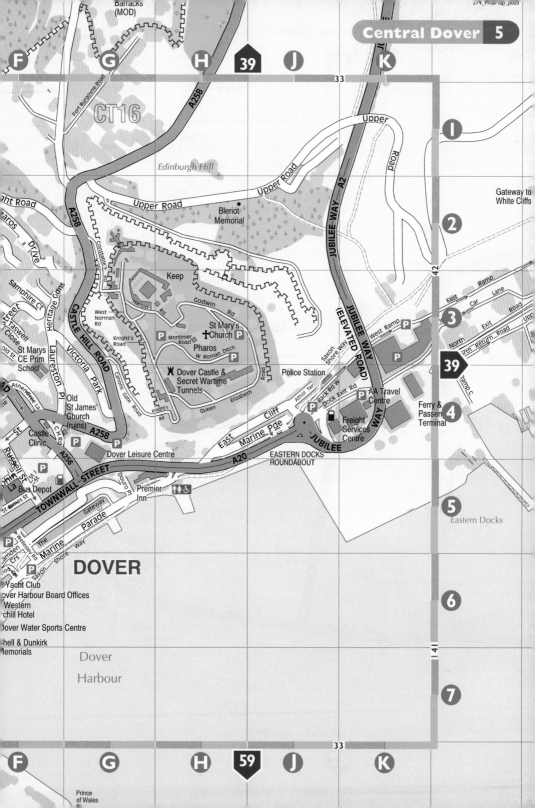

Barracks (MOD)

F **G** **H** 39 **J** **K**

CT16

Fort Burgoyne Road

A258

33

Upper Road

Upper Road

Edinburgh Hill

Bleriot Memorial

Upper Road A2

JUBILEE WAY

Gateway to White Cliffs

I

2

42

Keep

Harold's Rd

Godwin Rd

West Norman Rd

Constable's

St Marys CE Prim School

Laureston Pl

Heritage Gdns

CASTLE HILL ROAD

Victoria Park

Knight's Road

Mortimer Road

St Mary's Church

Pharos

W Roman Ditch

Dover Castle & Secret Wartime Tunnels

Canon's Gate Road

Knight's Rd

Queen Elizabeth

Cross Ditch Road

JUBILEE WAY (ELEVATED ROAD)

Saxon Shore Way

West Ramp

East Ramp

Car Lane

North Exit

Trn Return Road

Upr Road

3

39

Ramp C

Police Station

Ferry & Passen Terminal

4

P

P

P

AA Travel Centre

West Ramp

Athol Ter

Back Rd W

Dock Exit Rd

Freight Services Centre

JUBILEE WAY

samphire Ct

Traswell

Close

St Marys St

Ashenlree La

Old St James' Church (ruins)

A258

Castle Clinic

A256

C H Rd

Russell St

John St

St James St

Bus Depot

Camden Crs

Wellesley Rd

Saxon Shore Way

Douro Pl

Gateway

The Marine Parade

Dover Leisure Centre

TOWNWALL STREET

Premier Inn

Cliff

East Marine Pde

A20

EASTERN DOCKS ROUNDABOUT

5

Eastern Docks

DOVER

Yacht Club

over Harbour Board Offices

Western

chill Hotel

Dover Water Sports Centre

hell & Dunkirk Memorials

Dover

Harbour

141

6

7

33

F **G** **H** 59 **J** **K**

Prince of Wales

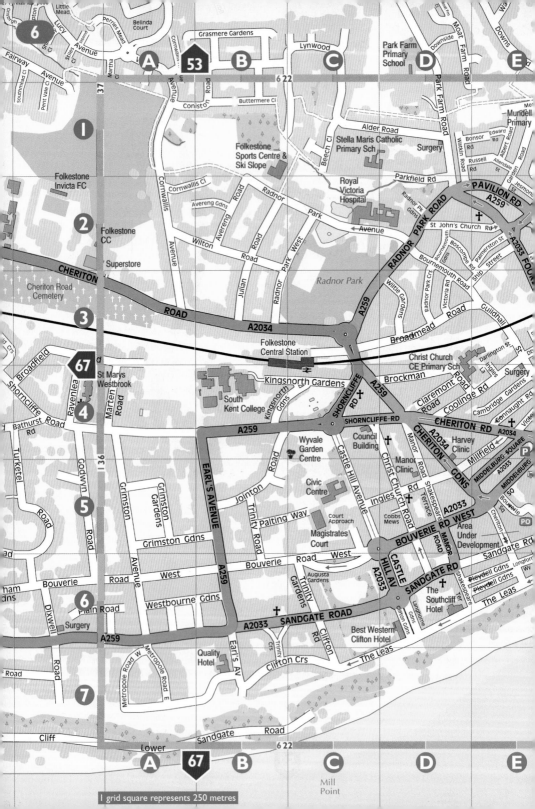

I grid square represents 250 metres

CANTER
Ethelbert
St Saviours Cl
Invicta Rd
Marshall
Greenfield Road
Green
Street
Road
Bowles
George Spurgen Comm Primar School

F
G
H
54
J
K

Canterbur Road
Crescent
Ernwell Rd
Archer
Dawson Rd
Bolton Road
Eastfields
Brambledown Rd
Eastfields

Denmark Street
Sidney
Bridge St
Alexandra St
Myrtle Rd
Ash Rd
Tree Elm Rd
Rd
Lawrence Ct
Stuart Road

Surgery
Telford's
Gladstone Rd

DOVER ROAD
SOUTHERN WY
LC

Highfield Industrial Estate
Martello Industrial Estate
Warren Close
Whitecliff Way
Way

I

Foreland Avenue

Warren
Nason
Neason
Way
Way

St Mary CE Primary School

2

Surgery
Morrison Rd
Folly Rd
Rossendale Gdns
Rossendale
Ormonde Rd
A260
Warren Rd
Bradley
Rd
Burrow Rd
Penfold Rd
Seagrave Crs
Crescent
Hasborough Rd
Bay

Martello Rd
DOVER RD
Abbott Rd
Grove Road
Lennard Road
Southbourne
Rd
Segrave Road
Bay
Varne Road
Varne Place
Road
Bay

Peter St
St John's Street
Queen Street
Radnor Bridge Rd
Ryland Pl
Dudley Road
East Cliff Road
E Cliff Passage
Wear
Wear

3

69

Charlotte St
Harvey St
Harvey Pl
Harbour Way
London St
Elmstead Pl
Radnor Br Rd
E Cliff Gdns

BRADSTONE RD
Clarence Rd
A2053
St Michael's Street
TONTINE ST
Cambridge Terrace
Mngr St
Sffrn's Pl
THE TRAM ROAD
Dyke Road
North St

4

Foord Rd S
CE Chapel Christian ool
DOVER
GRACE
HILL
Mill Bay
Payers Rendezvous
Keith Graham Academy
The Old High St
A260
St Eanswythe
er Screen ema
The Bayle
St Eanswythes CE Primary Sch
George Lane
The Bayle
Church St
Priory Gdns
The Durlocks
The
East St
Radnor St
Fish Market
St Peters CE Primary School
The Stade
Folkestone Yacht & Motor Boat Club

5

W Cliff Gdns
Albion Vls
Road of Remembrance
Radnor Cliff
Marine Crs
Marine Parade
MARINE TER
SANDGATE RD
Marine Parade Mews
Marine Pde
HARBOUR AD
MARINE PARADE
LWR
Beach St

6

Road

FOLKESTONE

7

F
G
H
68
J
K

10

634 | 51

A

Willow Road

Great Mongeham

Mongeham Church Close

B

Ashl Close

8
35

Mint Ind Est

C

St Nicholas Cl

St Martins Road

St Elizabeth carter Ave

St As Rd

St Francis Cl

Wilson Ave

St Richards Road

D

Clack Road

1

Sutton Lane

Pixwell La

Cherry Lane

Mongeham Road

Ellens Road

Mill Hil

St M
RC
Sch

Marlboroug
Industrial E

2

3

Sunnyside Close

Manties Hill

Church Lane

50

Sutton Lane

Chapel Lane

4

The Ripple School

Ripple

Ripplevale School

Coldb
Farm

Sutton Vale House

Vale Road

Pommeus Lane

Ripple Farm

Crooked

S Road

5

149
634

A

B

12

Ripple Court

Sutton Lane

C

Ripple Road

Coldblow Road

D

Co

35

12

634 | 49

A **B** 10 35 **C** **D**

Ripple Court

Sutton Lane

Ripple Road

Coldblow

1

Winkland Oaks Farm

Sutton Lane

Manor View

2

48

Hangman's Lane

Hangman's Lane

Front S

Back S

Queen's Rise

3

Appleton Manor

Ringwould Road

DOVER ROAD

4

Waterworks Lane

The Street

Lucerne Lane

5 Martin

Martin Mill Station

Station App

A258

Langdon Road

Lucerne Lane

Old Rom Road

634

A Station Road **B** 24 35 **C** **D** Gurtling

Hawthorn Farm Caravan Park

Martin Mill

1 grid square represents 500 metres

E   F   **II**   G   H

37   38   49

Ringwould

Kingsdown

Knights Bottom

Glen Road

Courtlands

Boundary Road

Cliffe Road

Wellington Parade

I

Claremont Road

Osborne Road

Balmoral Road

Balmoral Road

Edward Road

Church Cliff

Irv Pl

North Road

South Road

Sea

Carlton Road

King's Close

St Monicas Road

†

Kingsdown & Ringwould CE Prim School

Rise

Street

Undercliffe Road

2

The Alexandra Road

St James Road

Upper

PO

Ringwould Road

Chalk Hill Road

48

The Avenue

Kingsdown Hill

Walme Kingsdown Golf Club

3

Victoria Road

Hillcrest Road

Queensdown

Bayview Road

Northcote Road

Oldstairs Road

Oldstairs Road

The Leas

Hill Farm

47

4

Road

Granville Road

Golf Course

e Lynch

Free Down

Otty Bottom

5

E   F   **25**   G   H

37   38

Collingwood Road East

Hope Point

14

Pilgrims Way

Lane

A **B** **C** **D**

603 04

Bramble

Lane

1

Perry
Court
Farm

North Downs Way

47

B C

Wye Road

W
St

LC

**Kempe's
Corner**

Spring
Grove
School

Harville Road

2

3

Park B
Farm

CANTERBURY ROAD

A28

46

Wilmington
Farm

Great Stour

4

Kennington
Hall

Stour Valley Walk

◀**19**

5

145

E Mtn

xton
se

603 04

A28

Orchard Lane

A Valley Walk **B** **C** **D**

E   F   G   H

06   07

I

47

Olant

Wye Court

siness

Abbts Wk
Abbots Walk

Field Way

T First

Imperial College London

High Street

Church Street

Upper Bridge

Scotton Street

Street

PO
Old VC Con

T Ct

PH

Coldharbour   Lane

Street

anna
ll (End)
-Sch

Stonegate

PH

Cherry Garden La

C Ct

C Ct

Jarman's Field

Withersdane Hall

Coldharbour Farm

2

Wye Crown

W
Do

Little Chequers

S A Gn

Chequers Park

Orchard Dr

Wye

3

Oxenturn Road

Surgery

46

Amage

Ama
Far

Silks Farm

4

Withersdane

Oxenturn Road

5

145

06   07

E   F   G   H

The Street

16

595   46   96

Little Chart Forstal

and Way

Ram   Lane

1

West   Street

Rooting Street

Hoth Com

Greensand   Way

Hothfield Bogs

2

45

West   Street

Great   Stour

Stour Valley Walk

Hothfield Primary

3

Mitchell Farm

Betchersden Road

4

44

Stour Valley Walk

Betchersden Road

5

Stour Valley Walk

Pluckley Road

Ripper's Cross

Bear's Lane

595   96

1 grid square represents 500 metres

STONE ROAD

E

F

Works

G

H

98

99

46

I

A20

Ripple Court

Channel Tunnel Rail Link

Hothfield

Coach Drive

Pln Cl

Sch Cl

Beech Dr

Park Drive

Home Farm

Mill House

45

Waterfall

Road

2

Westwell Lane

3

18

Greensland Way

Godinton Lane

Greensland Way

4

144

Godinton House

5

Goldwyn Community Special School

Greensland Way

Spindlewood Dr

Whitebeam Cl

Erin Cl

Se La

E

F

G

28

H

98

99

Sweet Bay

Aspen Dr

Wild Gr

Holly Mow

Lilac Court

Butternut Copse

Mulberry Rd

Evrgrn Wy

Loudon Ct

Lou

Worten

Godinton Primary School

Stour Valley Walk

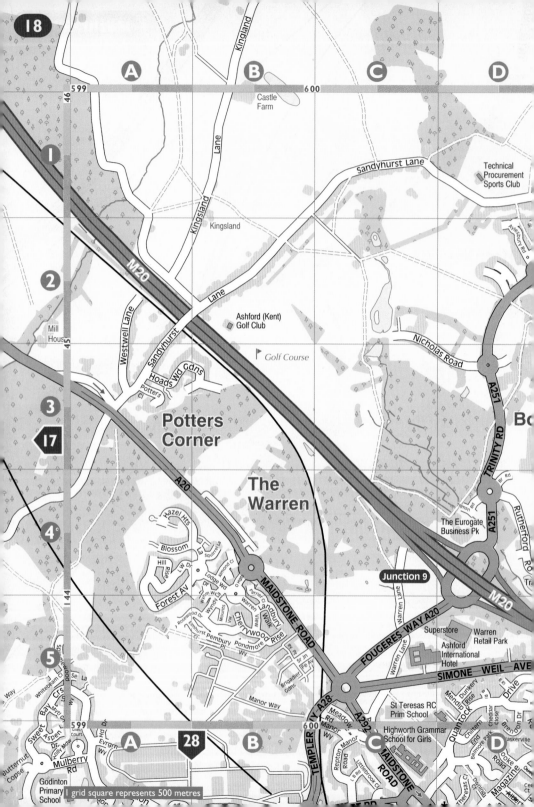

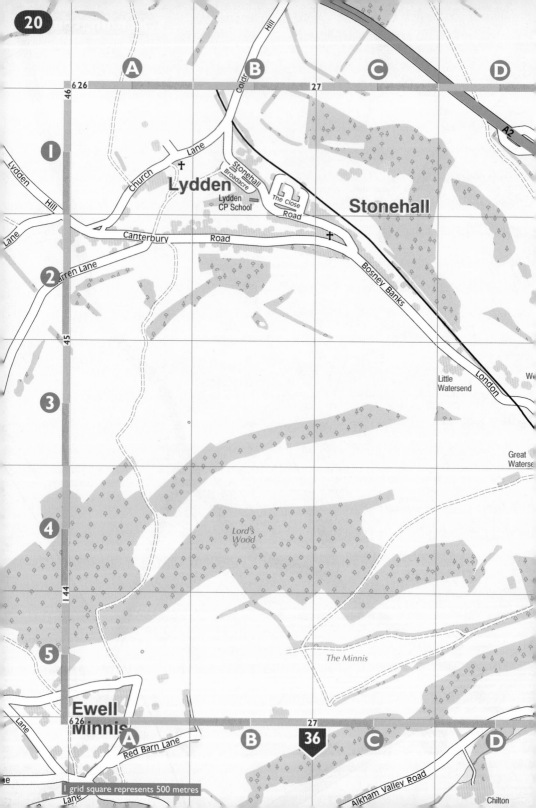

Holly Lodge

Beechwood Cl

E   F   G   H

29   30   46

Singledge Lane

Singledge

Temple Farm

Singledge Lane

Green Lane

Nursery

Lenacre La

Guilford Avenue

The Pier

The Acre

Lenacre Lane

Bewsbury Cross Lane

Beauxfield

Grace Meadow

Sandwich Road

Mayfield Road

Bewsbury Crescent

Castle Drive

Singledge Ave

Surgery

PO

Archer's Ct Rd

Ramada Hotel

A2

22

Honeywood

Kearboun Sq

Keyes

Bindon Blood Rd

France Road

Menzies Road

Willingdon

Temple Side

Temple Close

Target Firs

Temple Road

The Green

Avenue

Lane

Temple Ewell

London Road

Riverside

Watersend

Brookside

Temple Road

Mill St

PO

Wellington Rd

Park Rd

Malvern Meadow

Malvern Road

Egerton Road

Woodside

Laburnum Close

Whitfield Hill

A256

Mansion Gardens

Menzies Road

Palmerston Rd

Focal Point Rd

Temple Ewell CE Primary School

Scotland Common

Lower Ewell Road

Kearsney Station

Surgery

Surgery

London Road

C D

Close

Kearsney

Bushy Ruff House

Kearsney court

Alkham Road

Abbey Road

Kearsney Abbey

Pavilion Meadow Road

Chisnall

Sanctuary Close

Chilton Avenue

Coxhill Crescent

Minnis Lane

Meadway

Lower Road

Chilton Way

River Str

Beresford Road

River Dale

River CP School

Common

Lewis

Lewis Valley Road

LONDON ROAD

A256

Friars Way

Pilgrims Way

Shipmans Way

Old Pk

Crabble Corn Mill

E   F   **37**   G   H

29   30

I

2

3

4

5

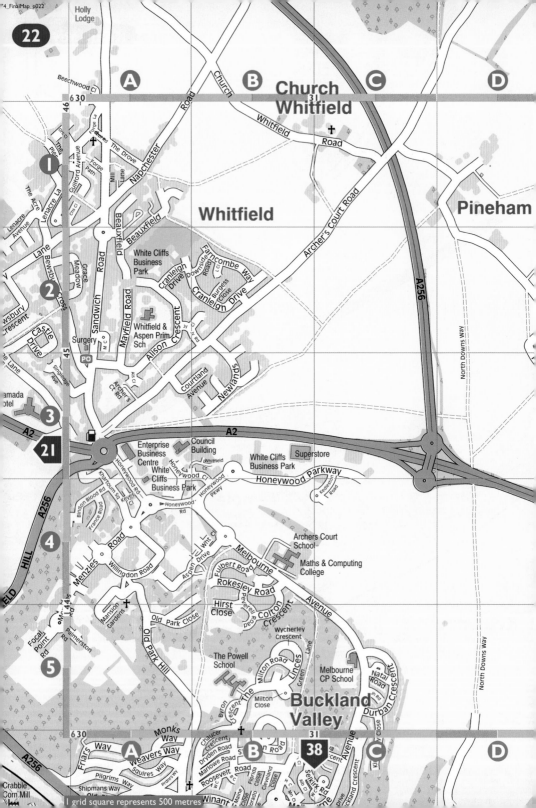

East
Langdon

School
West
Side
West
Side
East
Hawthorn Farm

E   F   G   H

The Street

33   34

I

Langdon Road

Solton Manor
Farm

2

24

45

A258

East Langdon Road

3

The Street

Guston

The Lane

Chance Meadow

Barnfye Close

Prescott Close

Hangman's Lane

The Lane

4

144

A2

St Martin's Road

Bere Farm

5

Dover

PO

Premier Inn

33   34

E   F   39   G   H

Gibraltar Square

Tangier Close

Dunkirk Square

24 Martin

Martin Mill Station

A

B

12

C

D

634

Langdon Road

Lucerne

Lane

Old Roman Road

Station Road

A258

Green

Curling Rd

East Farm

Hawthorn Farm Caravan Park

Martin Mill

I

46

Seymour Road

Nelson Park Road

Hardy Road

Collingwood

Station Road

2

St Vincent Road

olton Manor arm

3

Pond

Lane

23

45

A258

West Cliffe

Wallett's Court

Millfield

High

Townsend Farm Road

Well La

Vicarage Lane

4

Dover Road

Wallett's Court Country House Hotel

St Margaret's at Cliffe

St Georges Place

Reach

Roman Way

Re Clo

Glebe

Langdon Cl

DOVER ROAD

5

144

634

Reach Court Farm

Bere Farm

A

B

35

C

D

1 grid square represents 500 metres

Bottom

E   F   13   G   H

37   38

Hope Point

I

46

2

3

45

4

St Margaret's Bay

5

44

E   F   37   G   H   38

Collingwood Road East

Fleet Road

Norway

Drove

Road

Hog's Bush

Redown

The Droveway

Bockhill Farm

Granville Road

Saxon Shore Way

Saxon Shore Way

The Rise

Norman Road

The Droveway

Victoria Av

Road

Granville Road

St Margarets at Cliffe Prim Sch

Portal House School

Medical Cen

Convent Close

Kenilworth Cl

Droveway Gdns

Downside Cl

Salisbury Road

Granville Hill

Hotel Road

Clyngh Rd

Street

Bay Road

PH

M

The Pines Garden

The Bay Museum

St Margaret's Road

Beach Road

Road

Foreland Road

The Crescent

Shore Way

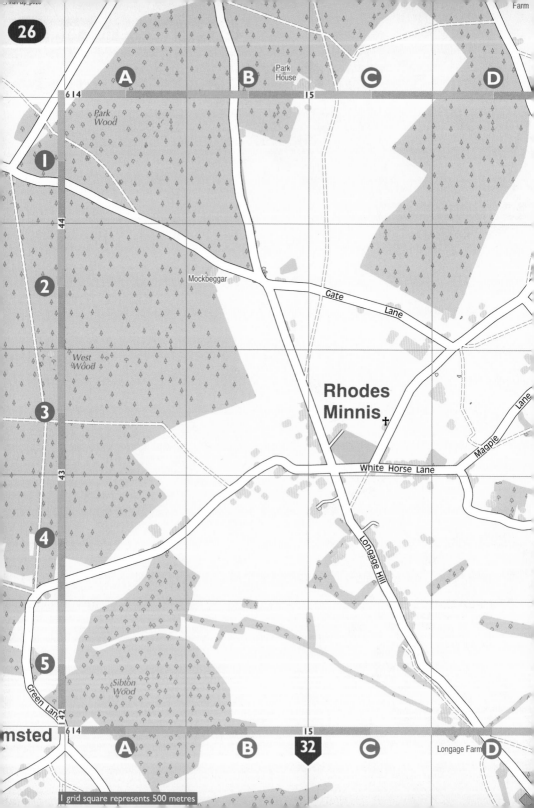

E   F   G   H

17

18

Rural Heritage
Centre

Exted

Park Lane

Fairfield

High Street

Elham

High
St

The Row

Cullen's Hl

Cherry
Gardens

Old
Hospital

Linden
Dr

PO

Cock La

Water
Farm

Cullens
Hl

Hnt Brk

New Rd

Prtd La

Duck Street

The Hart

Vicarage La

Surgery

Rd

Plo

Elham CE
Primary School

Hog Grn

Mount

Cemetery

Collards   Lane

Canterbury   Road

Elham Valley Way

Millhill Farm

Bereforstal
Farm

Boyke Lane

Ottinge

Canterbury   Road

Shuttlesfield   Lane

Elham Valley Way

Wic

I

44

2

3

43

4

42

5

E   F   **33**   G   H

17   18

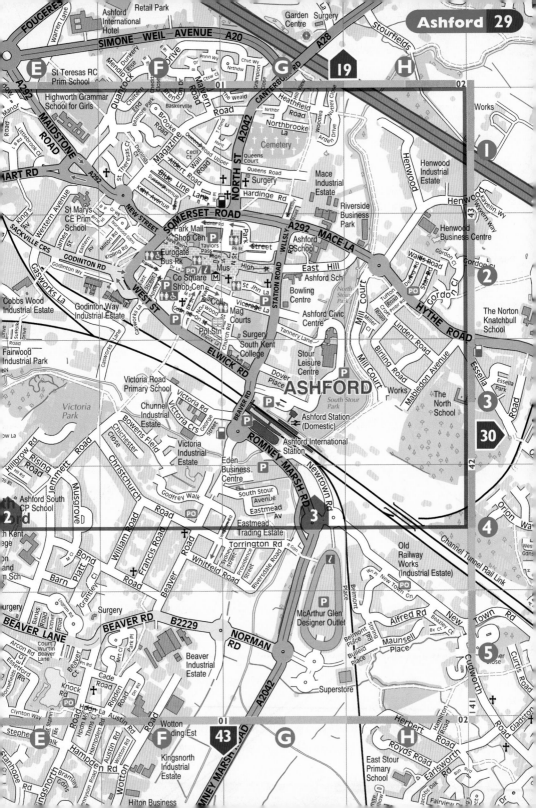

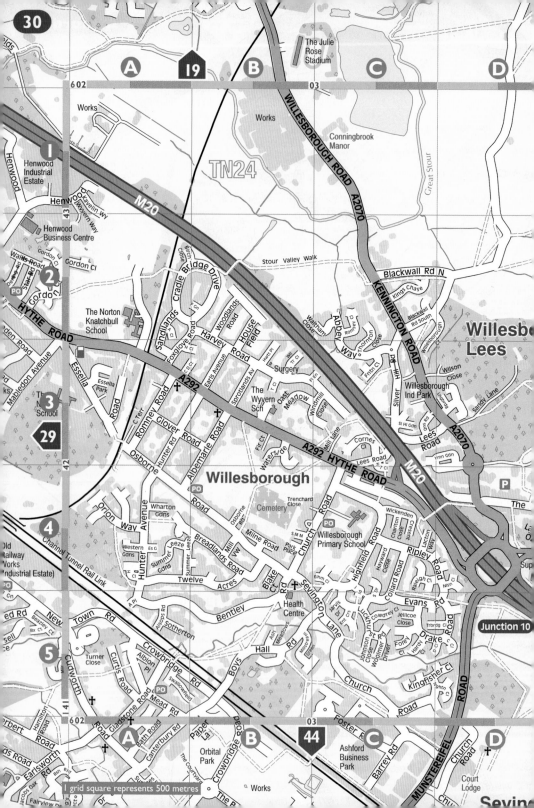

E   F   G   H

Primary
School

Spelders

Goodcheap
Farm

Goodcheap Lane

I

Plumpton
Farm

2

Hinxhill

3

William
Harvey
Hospital

Ouseley
Farm

Hinxhill Road

&E

4

Wyevale
Garden Centre

nmrhill
PK

Bockham Lane

Quarrington Lane

Quarrington
Farm

5

A20

HYTHE ROAD

45

E   F   G   H

eld Lane

32

Green Lane

msted

614

42

Sibton Wood

A

B

26
15

C

D

Longage Farm

Sibton
Schoo

1

Woodland

Woodland Road

2

Barton Fld

Bedingfield Wy

Brady R

Fox Cl

Ethelb
Driv

keete

41

Skeete Road

Brady Road

Palm Tra

3

Dog Kennel
Lane

Woodland
Road

Lyminge

ing
mon

4

Postling
Wood

Bro

North Downs Way

140

5

New

614

15

A

B

50

North L   y

C Staple Farm

D

I grid square represents 500 metres

Canterbury

Shuttlesfield Lane

Elham Valley Way

E

F

27

17

G

H

18

42

I

Yewtree
Cross

Great
Shuttlesfield
Farm

2

41

Canterbury Road

Church Rd

Surgery

Pleasant

Robus Cl

Wnt Cl

Well
Road

North Lyminge Lane

Elham Valley Way

The Sidings

Lyminge CE
Primary
School

PO

Nash Hill

Station Road

Greenbanks

Mayfield
Road

Rectory Lane

3

Surgery

reet

Elham Valley Way

4

140

Etchinghill
Golf Club

Leas Road

5

Valley Way

Saxon Shore Way

The
Orchids

Teddars

E

51

G

H

18

Saxon Shore Way

tchinghill

Tolsford Cl

Ivy Cl

Westfield Lane

St Mary's Cl

St Mary's

Canterbury Road

F

The Minnis

Ⓐ   Ⓑ   **20**   Ⓒ   Ⓓ

6 26   27

Lane

Ewell Minnis

Red Barn Lane

Alkham Valley Road

Chilton Farm

Ⓘ

Green Lane

43

2

Alkham Valley Road

Wolverton

Minnis Lan

short

Glebeland

3

42

4

Mount Ararat

St Radigund's Abbey

5

1 41

6 26   27

Poulton Farm

Copt Hill Farm

Ⓐ   Ⓑ   **56**   Ⓒ   Ⓓ

1 grid square represents 500 metres

Bushy Ruff House

Kearsney court

Kearsney Abbey

Alkham Road

Pavilion Meadow

Chisnall

Chilton Avenue

Abbey Road

E   **F**   **21**   **G**   LONDON ROAD   **H**

A256

Sanctu Close

Lower Road

River Street

River Dale

Coxhill Gardens

Chilton Way

Beresford Road

Crabble Corn Mill

Crescent

PO

Common Lane

Valley Road

Lewisham

Lower Road

Kingston Cl

Minnis Lane

Meadway

River CP School

Dove Lea Gardens

Bylan Road

Door Side

Mannering Close

Meadow River

Crabble Lane

Mill Close

M1 Race

Badgers Rise

River

Cowper

Hazeldown

Road

Orchard Drive

Luckhurst Road

Ash Close

Lyndhurst Road

Briar Close

Crabble Close

River Drive

Lewisham Rd

Crabble Avenue

2

T Sp

Hawthorn Close

Road

The Ridgeway

Wingrove Hill

Westdean Close

Woodland Close

Deanwood Road

Crabble

Crabble Lane

River Bottom Wood

St Radig Commun Primary

Close

3

Abbey Road

Holmestone Road

Coombe Road

Barwick Road

Beaufoy

38

PO

Coombe

Poulton Business Park

Hollow Wood Road

Poulton Close

Ind Estate

Whinless Road

Coombe Road

4

Queens Avenue

To Ha

Queens Aven

Elms

Harbour School

Elms Vale Road

Markland Road

Reading Road

5

St Martins School

Marlborough Road

St Martins Road

Eaves Road

E   **F**   **57**   **G**   **H**

Chilverton Elms

Elms Hill

Elms Vale Road

Elms Wood

Maxton

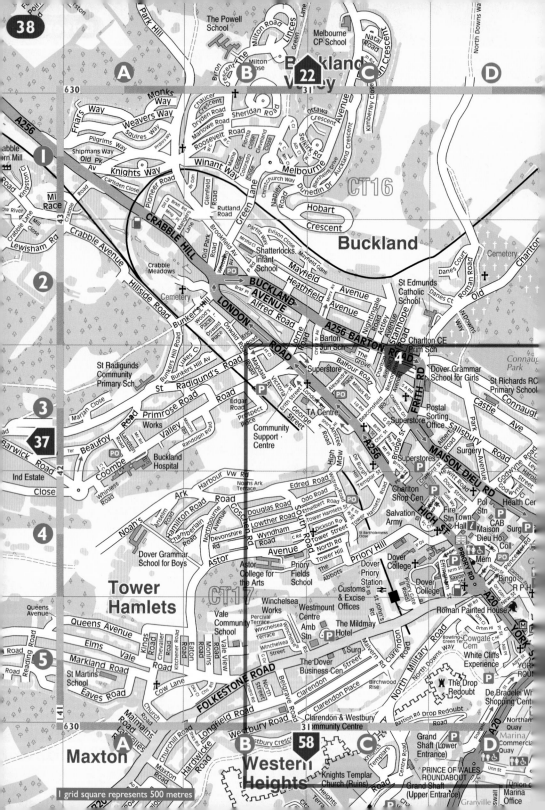

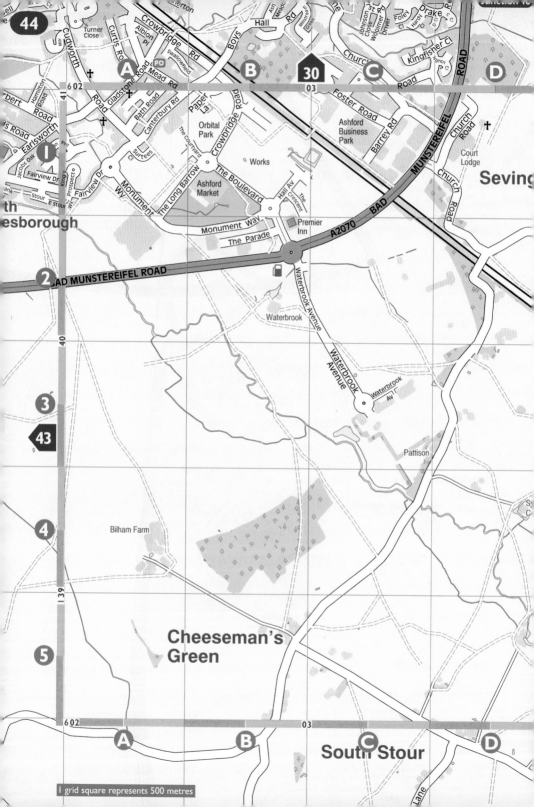

E F 31 G H

05 06 41

I

2

3

46

4

139 5

E F G H

05 06

A20

HYTHE ROAD

Bockhal

Highfield Lane

Kingsford Street

Blind Lane

Longthorne Farm

M20

A20

HYTHE ROAD

Glebelands

Old Rector Cl

The Orchids

Kingsford Street

Oaklands

PO

Mersham

Bower Road

nscience m

Jemmett Lane

The Forstal

Church Road

Church Cl

Orchard Cl

Cherry Glebe

Bower Road

Mersham Primary School

Denne

Channel Tunnel Rail Link

Little Stock Farm

ee Farm

Flood Street

Stonegreen Hall Farm

East Stour River

46

A   B   C   D

6 06   41   07

Bircholt
Court

1

Hatch
Park

Brockham
Farm

The Leet

2

Ridgeway

Woolpack

Sandy Pl

Smeeth
CP School

Caroland Cl

The   Ridgeway

Church Road

HYTHE ROAD

3

A20

Church Road

Smeeth

Home Farm

45

The Paddocks

HYTHE ROAD

†

Coldecott
School

Rd

Stock   Lane

4

M20

Station

Bower Road

Evegate Manor
Farm

Little
Stock
Farm

Evegate
Business
Centre

1 39

...unnel Rail Link

5

6 06   07

A   B   C   D

East Stour

I grid square represents 500 metres

E   F   G   H

09   10   41

I

Lees Road

Pound Lane

Pound Lane

Park Farm

Mountbatten Way

Canterbury Road

†

The Pound House

2

40

Brabourne Lees

spect Way

Knatchbull Way

Plain

†

Road

Pound Lane

Granary Court Rd

Southenay Farm

3

Ramstone Close

Manor Leaze

Lodge House

Lilyvale Road

Plain Road

Granary Court Road

Southenay Lane

4

Lilyvale

139   **48**

Barn

HYTHE ROAD

A20

Cooper's Lane

Stone Hill

Stone Hill

5

E   F   G   H

Stone Hill

ASHFORD   ROAD

09   10

†

M20

Works

†

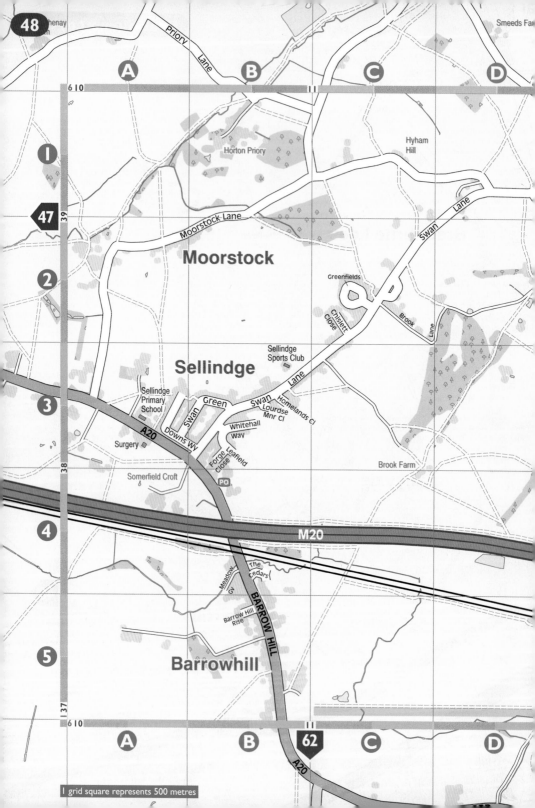

Priory Lane

A **B** **C** **D**

610 |1

Smeeds Far

henay

Horton Priory

Hyham
Hill

39

Moorstock Lane

Moorstock

Swan Lane

Greenfields

2

Chislett Close

Brook Lane

Sellindge

Sellindge
Sports Club

3

Sellindge
Primary
School

Swan Green

Swan Lane

Homelands Cl

A20

Downs Wy

Lourdse
Mnr Cl

Whitehall
Way

Surgery

Leafield Close

Brook Farm

38

Forge Close

Somerfield Croft

PO

4

M20

The
Cedars

Meadow
Gv

BARROW HILL

Barrow Hill
Rise

5

Barrowhill

137

610

A **B** **C** **D**

A20

1 grid square represents 500 metres

Monks
Horton
Manor

E

F

G

H

13

14

Blindhouse

I

Pent Farm

ndhouse Lane

STONE STREET

B2068

39

P

e Farm

Hayton
Manor

2

Hayton Road

3

50

Stanford

Ch F

Street

38

Yew Tree
Cl

4

Kennett Lane

Stone Street

B2068

Beckley
Pl

M20

Westenhanger
Station

Junction 11

5

B2068

ASHFORD ROAD

Folkestone
Racecourse

E

F

G

13

14

63

H

Westenhanger

eadow
Court

ROAD

A20

Sandling
Park

Sh

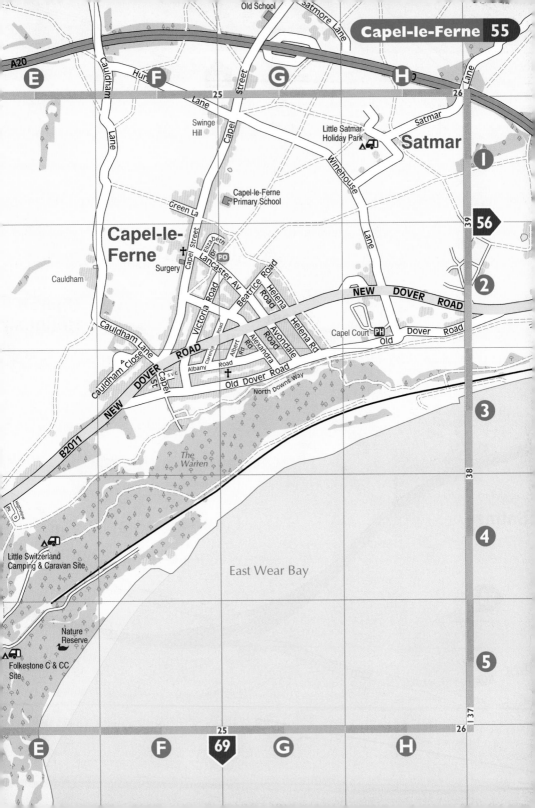

A20

E

Caudham Lane

Hur

F

Swinge Hill

Caudham

Green La

Old School

Satmore Lane

Street

Capel

Lane

25

Capel-le-Ferne Primary School

Capel-le-Ferne

Capel Street

Elizabeth Dr

PO

Surgery

Lancaster Av

Victoria Road

Beatrice Road

Helena Road

Clarence Road

Albert Rd

Alexandra Road

Albany Road

Avondale Road

Helena Rd

G

Little Satmar Holiday Park

Winehouse Lane

Satmar

Satmar

I

39

56

2

Cauldham Lane

NEW DOVER ROAD

Capel St

svc

Old Dover Road

North Downs Way

NEW DOVER ROAD

Capel Court

PH

Old Dover Road

Old

3

38

The Warren

4

Little Switzerland Camping & Caravan Site

East Wear Bay

Nature Reserve

Folkestone C & CC Site

5

B2011

NEW DOVER ROAD

37

Harbour School

Elms Road

Marlborough Road

Re

St Martins School

Eaves Road

E

F

37

29

G

H

30

41

Maxton

I

B2011

Rugby Road

Manor Ro

Manor

Chilverton Elms

Elms Hill

Elms Vale Road

Elms Wood

B2011 FOLKESTONE ROAD

Farthingloe

2

Ay

40

Aycliffe County Primary School

St Davids Ave

Old

3

58

North

Folkestone Rd

Hill

Premier Inn

A20

North Downs Way

4

39

Samphire Hoe Country Park

Samphire Hoe

5

ydden
out

E

F

29

G

H

30

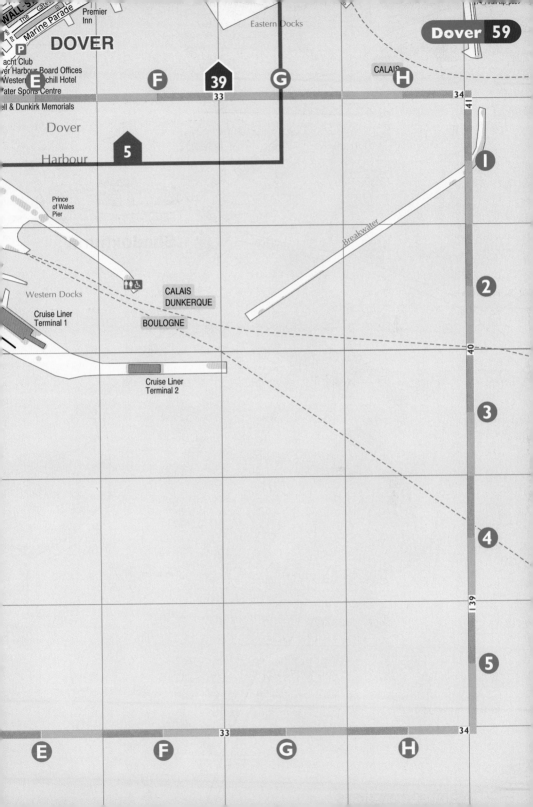

WALL ST.

The Gate

Marine Parade

Premier
Inn

P

DOVER

acht Club
er Harbour Board Offices
Western   chill Hotel
ater Sports Centre
ell & Dunkirk Memorials

Eastern Docks

CALAIS

E   **F**   **39**   **G**   **H**

33   34   41

Dover

Harbour   **5**

Prince
of Wales
Pier

Breakwater

Western Docks

CALAIS
DUNKERQUE

BOULOGNE

Cruise Liner
Terminal 1

Cruise Liner
Terminal 2

I

2

40

3

4

39

5

E   **F**   **G**   **H**

33   34

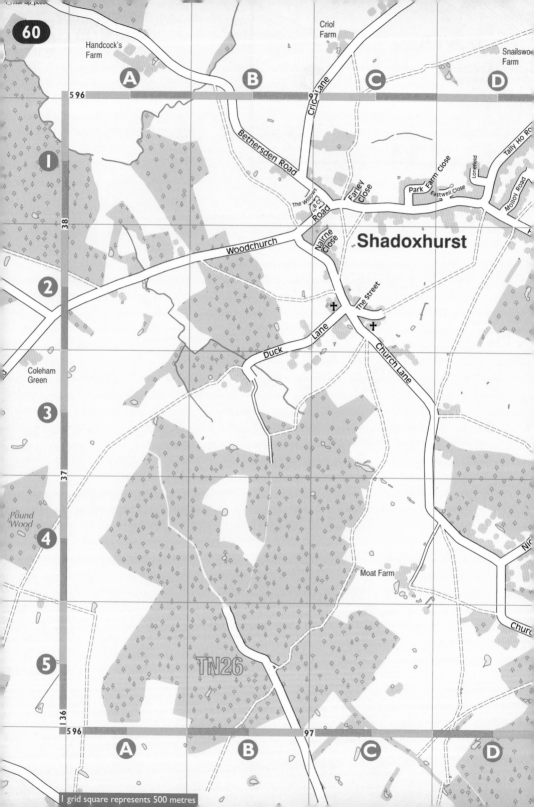

60

Handcock's Farm

Criol Farm

Snailswo Farm

596

Bethersden Road

Crio Lane

Park Farm Close
Eastwell Close
Lonefield
Tally Ho Ro
Mollon Road

The Willows

Farley Close

Road

1

38

Woodchurch

Nairne Close

Shadoxhurst

The Street

2

Duck Lane

Church Lane

Coleham Green

3

37

Pound Wood

4

Moat Farm

Nir

Churc

TN26

5

136

596

97

1 grid square represents 500 metres

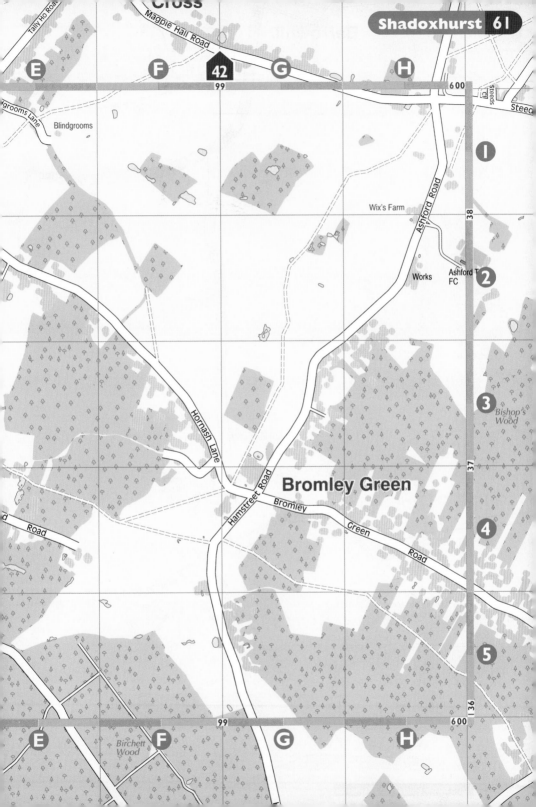

Cross

Magpie Hall Road

Tally Ho Road

E   **F**   **42**   **G**   **H**

99   **600**

Steed

Steed

grooms Lane

Blindgrooms

Ashford Road

I

38

Wix's Farm

Works   Ashford T
FC   **2**

Hornash Lane

3   Bishop's
Wood

37

Bromley Green

Hamstreet Road

Bromley

Green   Road   **4**

Road

5

136   600

99

E   **F**   **G**   **H**

Birchett
Wood

Barrowhill

A B 48 C D

HILL

A20

ASHFORD

Otterpool Manor

Upper Otterpool

Benh
Busir
Park

Harringe Brooks Wood

OTTERPOOL LANE

B2067

Lympne Industrial Estate

ALDINGTON ROAD

Aldington Road

Tourney

Beacon

Reach Road

Saxon Shore Way

Port Lympne Wild Animal Park, Mansion & Garden

Aldergate Wood

The Street

Ca

A Saxon Shore Way B C Stutfall Castle D

Royal Military Canal

610 37 I

36 2

3

135 4

610 5

1 grid square represents 500 metres

Folkestone C & CC
Site

Reserve

E   F   55   G   H

25   26   37

Copt
Point

I

2

36

3

4

I 35

5

25   26

E   F   G   H

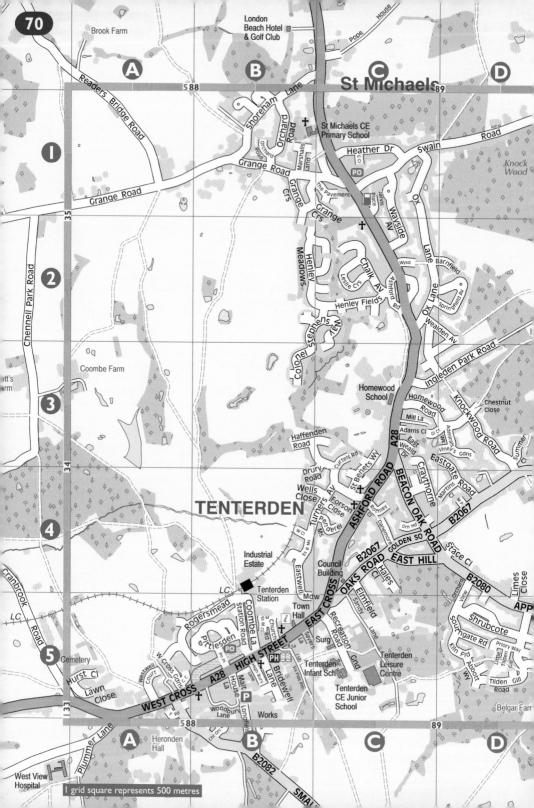

E   F   G   H

90   91

I

35

Swain Road

Huntbourne Farm

Swain Road

Swain Farm

2

Brissenden Farm

3

Old Knockwood

Golf Course

Tenterden Golf Club

RCH   ROAD

WOODCHURCH   ROAD

B2

34

The Dandy

4

Pigeon Hoo

ROAD

Judge Close

Collison Place

Finchden Manor

5

133

Leigh Green

90   91

E   F   G   H

Leigh Green Industrial

A · B · C · D

Hamstreet Road

Orlestone

Burnt Oak

Court Lodge Farm

A2070

Ashford Road

Hollybush Farm

Saxon Shore Way

National Nature Reserve

Ham Street Primary School

St Mary's Ch

Hamstreet Station

Larr Caster Cl

Bourne Lane

Bournewood

Bank Side

an orc

B2067

Old Mill

Carter's Wd

RUCKINGE RD

PO

Wrks

Broad

COCK LA

Surgery

Village Way

Willow Dr

Romney Rd

Hampden Farm

Meadow View Industrial Est

Burr Farm

WAREHORNE ROAD

B2067

Hamstreet

HAMSTREET ROAD

B2067

Mountain Farm

A2070

Saxon Shore Way

Wyevale Garden Centre

Marsh Rd

Royal Military Canal Path

A · B · C · D

Stonegate Farm

Dicker's Wood

E

F

G

H

I

Hill Fa

Saxon Shore Way

02

03

35

B2

2

34

Noakes Farm

nds

Herne House

Royal Military Canal Path

K

3

Ruckinge

Oak Rdg

ROAD

HAMSTREET

Fairview Industrial Park

Royal Military Canal Path

133

4

Hans Farm

5

Kitsbridge Lane

E

F

G

H

02

03

Lords Farm

A 63 B C 64 D

613 14

St M... Road

The Roughs

34

I

...erside ...ustrial Estate

The Haven

Burmarsh Road

Grebe Crs

Dove Cl

Kingfisher Av

Burmarsh Road

Wych

Elm Wy

C Rd

Peregrine Cl

Sy Cl

Romney-Hythe & Dym...

Kengat... Industri... Estate

Romney Way

Martello

Pennypot Industrial Estate

Shepherds Walk

Dymchurch Road

Martin's Wy

Robin's Cl

PO

Nightingale Av

Finch Gv

Meadow Way

A259

Crofters Cl

Pe...

Palmarsh

2

Heron's Wy

LC

Marsh View

Oaks View

Studfall Close

Palmbeach Avenue

Keddow's Close

St George's Place

Palmarsh Primary School

Jubilee Close

LC

• Hythe Ranges

3

33

4

Works

A259

5

Dymchurch Redoubt

132

613 14

A B C D

I grid square represents 500 metres

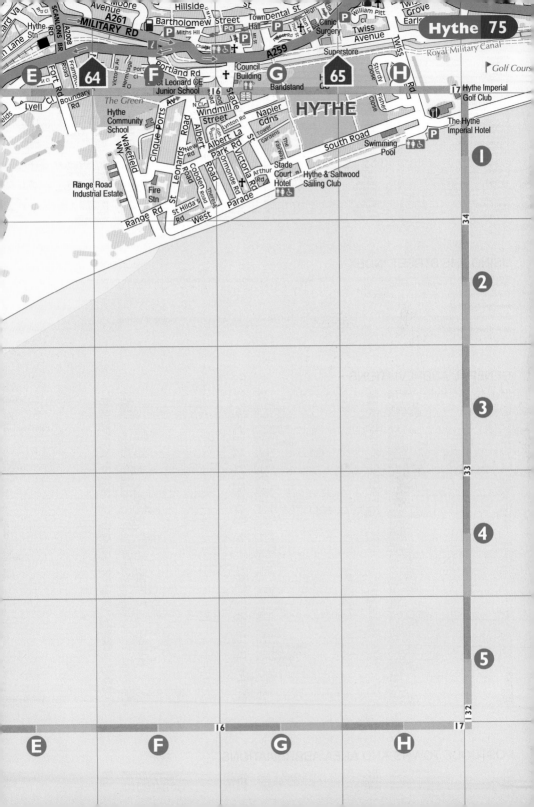

Arpinge 52 C1
Ashford 3 H6
Aycliff 58 A2
Barrowhill 48 A5
Berwick 63 E3
Bethersden 40 D2
Bockhanger 18 D3
Brabourne Lees 47 E2
Brissenden Green 41 E5
Broad Street 32 D4
Bromley Green 61 G4
Buckland 38 C2
Buckland Valley 22 B5
Bybrook 19 E4
Capel-le-Ferne 55 F2
Cheeseman's Green 44 A5
Cheriton 66 C1
Chilmington Green 42 A2
Church Hougham 56 D2
Coolinge 67 F3
Crabble 37 G2
Deal 9 G4
Densole 34 D1
Dover 5 G6
Elham 27 G1
Etchinghill 51 E1
Ewell Minnis 20 A5
Exted 27 F1
Farthingloe 57 H2
Folkestone 7 G6
The Forstal 45 F4
Frogholt 51 G4
Gibraltar 53 F1
Godinton Park 28 B2
Great Chart 28 A3
Great Mongeham 10 A1
Guston 23 E3
Hamstreet 72 A4
Hawkinge 35 E4
Hinxhill 31 F3
Horn Street 66 B3
Hothfield 17 E2
Hythe 75 G1
Kearsney 21 E5
Kempe's Corner 14 B2
Kennington 19 G3
Kingsdown 13 F2
Kingsnorth 43 E4
Leigh Green 71 F5
Lilyvale 47 F4
Little Chart Forstal 16 A1
Lydden 20 A1
Lyminge 32 D3
Lympne 63 E4
Martin Mill 24 A1
Maxton 58 A1
Mersham 45 G3
Mill Hill 10 D1
Moorstock 48 A2
Morehall 67 F1
Newbarn 32 D5
Newingreen 63 E2
Newington 51 H4
Ottinge 27 E5
Palmarsh 74 A2
Park Farm 43 G3
Pedlinge 63 H3
Peene 52 B3
Pennypot 74 D1
Pineham 22 D1
Postling 50 A2
Potters Corner 18 A3
Rhodes Minnis 26 C3
Ridgeway 46 C2
Ringwould 13 E2
Ripper's Cross 16 B5
Ripple 10 B4
River 37 F1
Ruckinge 73 G3
St Margaret's at Cliffe 24 C4
Saltwood 64 C3
Sandgate 67 E4
Satmar 55 H1
Seabrook 66 A5
Sellindge 48 A3
Sevington 44 D1
Shadoxhurst 60 C2
Sholden
Shorncliffe Camp
Singleton
Smeeth
South Ashford
South Willesborough
Stanford
Stanhope
Stonehall
Stone Hill
Stubb's Cross
Temple Ewell
Tenterden
Tower Hamlets
Upper Deal
Walmer
The Warren
West Cliffe
Westenhanger
Western Heights
West Hougham
Whitfield
Willesborough
Willesborough Lees
Withersdane
Wolverton
Woodland
Wye
Yewtree Cross

USING THE STREET INDEX

Street names are listed alphabetically. Each street name is followed by its postal town or area locality, the Postcode District, the page number, and the reference to the square in which the name is found.

Standard index entries are shown as follows:

Abbey Cl *DEAL* CT14 **9** E4

Street names and selected addresses not shown on the map due to scale restrictions are shown in the index with an asterisk:

Admirals Wk *HYTHE* CT21 * **75** G1

GENERAL ABBREVIATIONS

ACC	ACCESS
ALY	ALLEY
AP	APPROACH
AR	ARCADE
ASS	ASSOCIATION
AV	AVENUE
BCH	BEACH
BLDS	BUILDINGS
BND	BEND
BNK	BANK
BR	BRIDGE
BRK	BROOK
BTM	BOTTOM
BUS	BUSINESS
BVD	BOULEVARD
BY	BYPASS
CATH	CATHEDRAL
CEM	CEMETERY
CEN	CENTRE
CFT	CROFT
CH	CHURCH
CHA	CHASE
CHYD	CHURCHYARD
CIR	CIRCLE
CIRC	CIRCUS
CL	CLOSE
CLFS	CLIFFS
CMP	CAMP
CNR	CORNER
CO	COUNTY
COLL	COLLEGE
COM	COMMON
COMM	COMMISSION
CON	CONVENT
COT	COTTAGE
COTS	COTTAGES
CP	CAPE
CPS	COPSE
CR	CREEK
CREM	CREMATORIUM
CRS	CRESCENT
CSWY	CAUSEWAY
CT	COURT
CTRL	CENTRAL
CTS	COURTS
CTYD	COURTYARD
CUTT	CUTTINGS
CV	COVE
CYN	CANYON
DEPT	DEPARTMENT
DL	DALE
DM	DAM
DR	DRIVE
DRO	DROVE
DRY	DRIVEWAY
DWGS	DWELLINGS
E	EAST
EMB	EMBANKMENT
EMBY	EMBASSY
ESP	ESPLANADE
EST	ESTATE
EX	EXCHANGE
EXPY	EXPRESSWAY
EXT	EXTENSION
F/O	FLYOVER
FC	FOOTBALL CLUB
FK	FORK
FLD	FIELD
FLDS	FIELDS
FLS	FALLS
FM	FARM
FT	FORT
FTS	FLATS
FWY	FREEWAY
FY	FERRY
GA	GATE
GAL	GALLERY
GDN	GARDEN
GDNS	GARDENS
GLD	GLADE
GLN	GLEN
GN	GREEN
GND	GROUND
GRA	GRANGE
GRG	GARAGE
GT	GREAT
GTWY	GATEWAY
GV	GROVE
HGR	HIGHER
HL	HILL
HLS	HILLS
HO	HOUSE
HOL	HOLLOW
HOSP	HOSPITAL
HRB	HARBOUR
HTH	HEATH
HTS	HEIGHTS
HVN	HAVEN
HWY	HIGHWAY
IMP	IMPERIAL
IN	INLET
IND EST	INDUSTRIAL ESTATE
INF	INFIRMARY
INFO	INFORMATION
INT	INTERCHANGE
IS	ISLAND
JCT	JUNCTION
JTY	JETTY
KG	KING
KNL	KNOLL
L	LAKE
LA	LANE
LDG	LODGE
LGT	LIGHT
LK	LOCK
LKS	LAKES
LNDG	LANDING
LTL	LITTLE
LWR	LOWER
MAG	MAGISTRATES'
MAN	MANSIONS
MD	MEAD
MDW	MEADOWS
MEM	MEMORIAL
MI	MILL
MKT	MARKET
MKTS	MARKETS
ML	MALL
MNR	MANOR
MS	MEWS
MSN	MISSION
MT	MOUNT
MTN	MOUNTAIN
MTS	MOUNTAINS
MUS	MUSEUM
MWY	MOTORWAY
N	NORTH
NE	NORTH EAST
NW	NORTH WEST
O/P	OVERPASS
OFF	OFFICE
ORCH	ORCHARD
OV	OVAL
PAL	PALACE
PAS	PASSAGE
PAV	PAVILION
PDE	PARADE
PH	PUBLIC HOUSE
PK	PARK
PKWY	PARKWAY
PL	PLACE
PLN	PLAIN
PLNS	PLAINS
PLZ	PLAZA
POL	POLICE STATION
PR	PRINCE
PREC	PRECINCT
PREP	PREPARATORY
PRIM	PRIMARY
PROM	PROMENADE
PRS	PRINCESS
PRT	PORT
PT	POINT
PTH	PATH
PZ	PIAZZA
QD	QUADRANT
QU	QUEEN
QY	QUAY
R	
RBT	ROUNDA
RD	
RDG	
REP	REF
RES	RESE
RFC	RUGBY FOOTBALL
RI	
RP	
RW	
S	
SCH	SC
SE	SOUTH
SER	SERVICE
SH	
SHOP	SHO
SKWY	SK
SMT	SU
SOC	SC
SP	
SPR	S
SQ	SQ
ST	S
STN	ST
STR	ST
STRD	ST
SW	SOUTH
TDG	TR
TER	TER
THWY	THROUG
TNL	TU
TOLL	TO
TPK	TUR
TR	
TRL	
TWR	T
U/P	UNDER
UNI	UNIVE
UPR	U
V	
VA	V
VIAD	VIA
VIL	
VIS	
VLG	VI
VLS	V
VW	
W	
WD	W
WHF	W
WK	
WKS	W
WLS	W
WY	
YD	
YHA	YOUTH H

POSTCODE TOWNS AND AREA ABBREVIATIONS

ASH	Ashford (Kent)
DEAL	Deal
DVE/WH	Dover east/Whitfield
DVW	Dover west
FOLK	Folkestone
FOLKN	Folkestone north
HDCN	Headcorn
HYTHE	Hythe
KEN/WIL	Kennington/Willesborough
RASHE	Rural Ashford east
RASHW	Rural Ashford west
RCANTW	Rural Canterbury west
RDV	Rural D
RFOLK	Rural Folkes
TENT	Tente

A

...Cl DEAL CT14......9 E4
...Rd DVE/WH CT16......21 F5
...CT17......37 G3
...CT17......36 D3
...s Wk HYTHE TN21 *......15 E1
...bots DVW CT17......4 B4
...Wy TENT TN30......70 D5
...cl ASH TN23......7 G2
...cl DVE/WH CT16......21 H1
...m Cl DEAL CT14......70 C3
...em Cl DEAL CT14......28 B5
...als Wk HYTHE TN21 *......75 C1
...T TN30......70 D3
...alty Ms DEAL CT14......4 E6
...St DVW CT17......4 E6
...rome Rd RFOLK CT18......54 B5
...le Cl FOLK CT19......53 G5
...ci RDV CT15......39 F2
...Pl DVW CT17......4 E5
...Rd RFOLK CT18......55 F3
...arle Rd KEN/WIL TN24......30 B4
...Av DVE/WH CT16......38 B1
...La HYTHE CT21......64 D5
...Rd DEAL CT14......4 D2
...WH CT16......4 D2
...cl FOLK CT19......7 G5
...THE CT19......7 G5
...WIL TN24......3 F2
... Mews Rd FOLK CT20......7 F5
... Pl KEN/WIL TN24......30 A5
... Rd DEAL CT14......9 H1
...KN CT19......7 G5
...Vis FOLK CT20......7 F5
... Wy KEN/WIL TN24......19 E2
...KN CT19......7 G5
...arton Rd HYTHE CT21......62 A4
...emble Cl RASHE TN25......19 G4
...ci RASHE TN25......70 D5
...Rd KEN/WIL TN24......30 A5
...ter La DEAL CT14......9 H1
...Hts RFOLK CT18......53 E1
...Dr KEN/WIL TN24......19 E2
...cl RASHE TN25......38 A4
...nius Ct ASH TN23......43 E2
...Crs FOLK CT15......39 E2
...ci RFOLK CT18......35 E5
...dore Crs FOLK CT19 *......7 G5
...dore Rd TENT TN30......70 D5
...ci DVW CT17......58 A1
...y St ASH TN23......28 C5
...llfe Rd DVW CT17......58 G2
...rs Court Rd DVE/WH CT16......22 A3
...ry Sq DEAL CT14......11 H1
...ci ASH TN23......29 E5
...Dr KEN/WIL TN24......19 H4
...t Av DEAL CT14......9 G5
...ton Av......2 A6
...y Rd DEAL CT14......11 E1
...THE CT17......7 G1
...st FOLK CT19......7 G1
...orne Rd RFOLK CT18......19 F3
...urton Cl KEN/WIL TN24......30 A2
...cl DVW CT17......37 G1
... Tree La DVE/WH CT16......45 E4
...cl RASHE TN25......62 D4
...ce TN21......47 F5
...SHE TN26......61 H2
...VT TN30......70 D4
...e RDV CT15......24 D2
...Av FOLKN CT19......67 E1
...y Mill Cots FOLKN CT19 *......30 B5
...ndw KEN/WIL TN24......8 B5
...cn Cl DEAL CT14......9 H1
...ree Rd FOLKN CT19......7 H1
...ct ASH TN23......28 B1
...cl Dr ASH TN23......28 A1
...E/WH CT16......22 A4
...y Av DVE/WH CT16......38 C2
...Ct DVW CT17......38 C2
...Dr DVW CT17......9 G4
...ci DEAL CT14......11 G2
...stan Pl DEAL CT14......11 F3
...stan Rd FOLKN CT19......54 B5
...ci Rd ASH TN23......28 D5
...Ter DVE/WH CT16......2 E1
...ci......J4
...son Wk KEN/WIL TN24......19 H4
...and Crs DVE/WH CT16......4 D2
...ry Rd FOLK CT20......67 F2
...sta Gdns FOLK CT20......6 C6
...stus Wk ASH TN23......42 D3
...tus Cl ASH TN23......43 E3
...ns Orch TENT TN30 *......7 F7
...cl RASHE TN25......29 F5
...e Rd DVE/WH CT16......4 C1
...venue DEAL CT14......9 G2

DEAL CT14......13 G2
DVE/WH CT16......21 G4
RDV CT15......24 D4
Avereng Gdns FOLK CT19......6 A2
Avereng Rd FOLK CT19......6 A2
Avondale Rd RFOLK CT18......55 G2
Aylesbury Rd RASHE TN25......18 D2
Aylesford Pl DVE/WH CT16......30 A5
Ayrshire Cl KEN/WIL TN24......19 E2

B

Back Rd West DVE/WH CT16......5 J4
Back St DEAL CT14......12 D2
Badgers Den ASH TN23......28 B5
Badgers Ri DEAL CT14......11 CA
  DVW CT17......37 F1
Badlesmere Rd ASH TN23......42 C1
Baileys Fld ASH TN23......43 F2
Bad Munstereifel Rd ASH TN23......43 A6
Baker Rd FOLK CT19......67 E1
Baldric Rd FOLK CT20......67 F2
Baldwin Ter FOLK CT19......7 G1
Balfour Rd DEAL CT14......11 H1
  DVE/WH CT16......4 B1
Ball La RASHE TN25......19 G2
Balmoral Rd DEAL CT14......13 G1
Bamford Wy DEAL CT14......9 G5
Bank Side RASHW TN26......72 A4
Banks Rd ASH TN23......29 F5
Bank St ASH TN23......3 F4
  HYTHE CT21......65 G3
Bargates ASH TN23......42 C1
Barley Cl RASHE TN25......12 A5
Barley Wy ASH TN23......42 B2
Barnberry Cl ASH TN23......28 B5
Barnett Rd ASH TN23......28 D4
Barnfield TENT TN30......70 C2
Barnfield Rd FOLKN CT19......54 A5
Barnhurst La RFOLK CT18......34 D4
Barn Platt ASH TN23......28 A2
Barntye Ct RDV CT15......23 E5
Barrack Hl HYTHE CT21......64 D5
Barrey Rd KEN/WIL TN24......44 C1
Barrow Hl ASH TN23......3 E5
  RASHE TN25......48 D4
Barrow Hill Cots ASH TN23......48 D3
Barrow Hill Ri RASHE TN25......48 D5
Barrow Hill Ter ASH TN23......2 E1
Bartholomew Cl HYTHE CT21......64 D5
Bartholomew Gdns HYTHE CT21 *......64 D5
Bartholomew La HYTHE CT21......64 C4
Bartholomew St DVE/WH CT16......64 C1
  HYTHE CT21......64 D5
Barton Fld RFOLK CT18......32 D2
Barton Rd DVE/WH CT16......38 C2
Barton View Ter DVW CT17......37 H1
Barwick Rd DVW CT17......37 H3
Baskerville KEN/WIL TN24......3 H1
Bassett Cl FOLK CT20......65 F3
Bassett Gdns HYTHE CT21......4 C7
Bastion Rd DVW CT17......37 G4
Bath Ms KEN/WIL TN24 *......44 C1
Bath Rd KEN/WIL TN24......44 C1
Bathurst Rd FOLK CT20......67 G2
Battery Point HYTHE CT21......66 B5
Battle of Britain Flats DVW CT17 *......4 B1
Baxendale Ct KEN/WIL TN24......29 H1
Bay Hl RDV CT15......25 E3
Bayle St FOLK CT20......7 G4
The Bayle FOLK CT20......7 G4
Bayview Rd DEAL CT14......13 G3
Beachborough Rd FOLKN CT19......67 D1
Beach Rd RDV CT15......25 F5
Beach St DEAL CT14......9 H4
  FOLK CT19......7 G4
The Beach DEAL CT14......11 H1
Beacon Oak Rd TENT TN30......70 C2
Beaconsfield Av DVE/WH CT16......4 C1
Beaconsfield Rd DEAL CT14......4 B2
  DVE/WH CT16......4 B2
Beacon Wy HYTHE CT21......62 D4
Bean Cl ASH TN23......28 B5
Bear's La RASHW TN26......16 C5
Beatrice Hills Cl KEN/WIL TN24......19 G4
Beatrice Rd RFOLK CT18......55 G2
Beatty Rd FOLK CT19......54 B4
Beatty Rd FOLK CT19......7 G1
Beauchamp Av DEAL CT14......11 E1
Beauchamp Rd KEN/WIL TN24......30 A5
Beaufoy Rd DVW CT17......38 A3
Beaufoy Ter DVW CT17......37 H3
Beaufield DVE/WH CT16......4 C1
Beaver Ct ASH TN23......29 E5
Beaver La ASH TN23......28 C4
Beaver Rd ASH TN23......3 F7
Beazley Ct KEN/WIL TN24......29 H5
Becket Cl DEAL CT14......9 H2
Beckley Pl RASHE TN25......49 H4
Beckwith Gn FOLK CT20 *......67 E2
Bedingfield Wy RFOLK CT18......32 D2
Beech Cl DEAL CT14......9 C1
Beech Dr RASHW TN26......16 C5
Beechome Dr KEN/WIL TN24......19 E4
Beechwood Av FOLK CT20......6 A2
Beechwood Ct DEAL CT14......9 F5
Belcaire Ct HYTHE CT21......63 E4
Belgrave Rd DVW CT17......4 A5
Belinda Ct FOLKN CT19......53 H5
Bell Chapel Cl ASH TN23......28 C2
Bellevue St FOLK CT20......7 G3
Bells La TENT TN30......70 B5
Belmont Dr DEAL CT14......11 F3
Belmont Pl DVE/WH CT16......4 B1
Belmont Rd KEN/WIL TN24......30 A5
Belmore Pk KEN/WIL TN24......2 E1
Bench St DVW CT17......5 J4
Benson La RFOLK CT18......34 C5
Bensted ASH TN23......28 B1
Bentley Rd ASH TN23......3 F5
Beresford Rd DVW CT17......37 H3
Berkeley Cl FOLKN CT19 *......53 H5
The Berries RFOLK CT18......35 E5
Berwick La HYTHE CT21......64 A4
Bethany Cl DEAL CT14......9 G4
Bethersden Rd RASHW TN26......16 C5
Bewsbury Crs DVE/WH CT16......21 H2

Bewsbury Cross La DVE/WH CT16......21 H2
Biggin St DVE/WH CT16......5 H3
Biggins Wood Rd FOLKN CT19......52 D5
Billington Gdns KEN/WIL TN24......19 G3
Bindon Blood Rd DVE/WH CT16......22 A4
Birch Cl KEN/WIL TN24......30 A2
Birch Vis FOLK CT20 *......66 A4
Birchwood Rd DVW CT17......4 C6
Birdwood Av DEAL CT14......9 A4
Birkdale Dr FOLKN CT19......53 G4
Birling Rd KEN/WIL TN24......35 H5
Bishopsden ASH TN23......28 B5
Bishopswood ASH TN23......43 G4
Bittern Cl RFOLK CT18......53 C1
Black Bull Rd FOLKN CT19......7 F2
Blackdown Dr KEN/WIL TN24......18 D5
Blackhouse Hl RFOLK CT18......65 C5
Blackhouse Ri HYTHE CT21......65 C5
Blackthorn Wy ASH TN23......43 G4
Blackwall Rd North
  KEN/WIL TN24......3 G3
Blackwall Rd South
  KEN/WIL TN24......30 C2
Blake Cl DEAL CT14......11 F4
Blake Ct KEN/WIL TN24......30 A5
Bland Dr RFOLK CT18......35 E4
Blenheim Dr DVE/WH CT16......38 C1
  RFOLK CT18......54 D5
Blenheim Pl DEAL CT14......67 F3
Blenheim Rd DEAL CT14......9 F4
Blindgrooms La RASHW TN26......61 E1
Blindhouse La RASHE TN25......49 E1
Blind La ASH TN23......28 A5
Bloomsbury Wy KEN/WIL TN24......18 D3
Blossom La RASHE TN25......18 A4
Bluebell Cl ASH TN23......43 F3
Bluebell La ASH TN23......43 F3
Blue Fld ASH TN23......28 D5
Blue House La HYTHE CT21......50 D4
Blue Line La KEN/WIL TN24......3 F1
Blythe Ct HYTHE CT21 *......65 F5
Bockham La RASHE TN25......31 G5
Bockhanger La KEN/WIL TN24......19 F3
Bodenham Rd FOLK CT20......67 G3
Bolton Rd FOLKN CT19......7 H1
Bond La ASH TN23......43 E5
Bond Rd ASH TN23......29 E4
Bonsor Rd FOLKN CT19......6 D1
Boresisle TENT TN50 *......70 C2
Bonnefields ASH TN23......29 E4
Boscombe Rd DEAL CT14......6 D5
Bosney Banks RDV CT15......20 C2
Boston Cl DVE/WH CT16......38 D1
The Boulevard KEN/WIL TN24......44 B1
Boundary Rd DEAL CT14......13 H1
  HYTHE CT21......75 E1
Bourne La RASHW TN26......72 B3
Bournemouth Gdns FOLKN CT19......6 D2
Bournemouth Rd FOLKN CT19......6 D2
Bournewood RASHW TN26......72 B4
Bouverie Rd West FOLK CT20......6 E5
Bouverie Sq FOLK CT20......6 E5
Bowden Crs FOLK CT19......6 A1
Bowen Rd FOLKN CT19......67 F1
Bowers Fld ASH TN23......2 D1
Bower Rd RASHE TN25......45 G5
Bowles Well Gdns FOLKN CT19......54 D5
Bowling Green La DEAL CT14......9 F4
Bowling Green Ter DVW CT17......4 D5
Bowser Cl DEAL CT14......9 H2
Boxley ASH TN23......2 A2
Boyke La RCANTW CT4......27 E4
Boyne Rd RDV CT15......25 E1
Boys Hall Rd KEN/WIL TN24......54 C4
Brabner Ct FOLK CT19 *......54 C4
Brabourne Gdns FOLK CT20......67 E2
Bracken Cl KEN/WIL TN24......19 E3
Bradbridge Gn ASH TN23......28 B4
Bradfield Rd RASHE TN25......18 D4
Bradley Rd FOLK CT19......7 G2
Bradstone Av FOLKN CT19......7 F3
Bradstone New Rd FOLK CT20......7 F3
Bradstone Rd FOLK CT20......7 F3
Brady Rd RFOLK CT18......32 C3
Bramble Cl RASHE TN25......14 D1
Brambledown FOLK CT19......7 H4
Bramble La RASHE TN25......14 C5
Bramley Crs FOLK CT20......67 E2
Bramley Gdns ASH TN23......43 E1
  DVE/WH CT16 *......21 H1
Branch St DVW CT17......4 D5
Breadlands Cl KEN/WIL TN24 *......30 A5
Breadlands Rd KEN/WIL TN24......30 A5
Brecon Ri KEN/WIL TN24......18 D5
Bredgar Cl ASH TN23......42 D1
Brenchley Av DEAL CT14......9 G5
Brenchley Cl ASH TN23......42 C1
Brendon Dr KEN/WIL TN24......3 F1
Brentwood ASH TN23......42 C1
Brewer's Hl FOLK CT20......66 D4
Brewer St DEAL CT14......9 H2
Briar Cl DVW CT17......37 F1
  KEN/WIL TN24......19 E4
  RASHE TN25 *......14 D1
Bridewell La TENT TN30......70 C5
Bridge Cl HYTHE CT21......64 C5
Bridge Hl DEAL CT14......8 A1
Bridgeman Ct HYTHE CT21 *......64 D5
Bridge Rd ASH TN23......2 E1
  DEAL CT14......13 G1
  RASHE TN25......46 D2
Bridgeside DEAL CT14......9 G3
Bridge St DVE/WH CT16......4 D1
  FOLK CT19......7 H1
  RASHE TN25......14 D2
Bridle Wy HYTHE CT21......66 A4
Brideway La ASH TN23......28 D5
Brigadier Gdns ASH TN23......18 B5
Brisley Cl ASH TN23......42 B1
Brisley Ct ASH TN23......42 B1
Britannia La ASH TN23......42 A1
Britannia Rd DEAL CT14......9 H1
Britten Cl HYTHE CT21......64 C4
Broad RASHW TN26......72 B4
Broadacre RDV CT15......20 B3
Broadfield Cl FOLK CT20......67 G2
Broadfield Crs FOLK CT20......67 G2
Broadhurst Dr KEN/WIL TN24......19 F2
Broadmead ASH TN23......42 C1
Broadmead Rd FOLKN CT19......6 D3

Broadsole La RDV CT15......56 A2
Broad St DVE/WH CT16......9 H3
Broadview FOLK CT20......66 C3
Brockhill Rd HYTHE CT21......64 C4
Brockman Rd FOLK CT20......6 D4
Bromley Green Rd RASHW TN26......61 G4
Brook Cl HYTHE CT21......64 D4
Brooke Rd KEN/WIL TN24......3 F1
Brookfield Av DVE/WH CT16......38 B2
Brookfield Pl DVE/WH CT16......38 B2
Brookfield Rd ASH TN23......38 A7
  DVE/WH CT16......38 A1
Brook La RASHE TN25......48 C2
Brookside DVE/WH CT16......21 E4
Broomfield KEN/WIL TN24......30 D4
Broomfield Rd FOLKN CT19......67 E1
Broughton Ct ASH TN23 *......28 C5
Browning Pl FOLKN CT19......54 C5
Bruce Cl DEAL CT14......9 F5
Brunswick Gdns DVE/WH CT16......38 B1
Brunswick Rd ASH TN23......2 A3
Brunswick St DEAL CT14 *......3 F5
Bryony Dr ASH TN23......43 G4
Buckland Av DVE/WH CT16......38 B2
Bucksford La ASH TN23......28 A5
Buffs Av FOLK CT20......66 B1
Bulleid Pl KEN/WIL TN24......40 A3
Bull La RASHW TN26......40 A3
Bulls Cots HYTHE CT21 *......64 D5
Bullwark St DVW CT17......58 C1
The Bull Yd ASH TN23 *......3 F5
The Bulrushes ASH TN23......28 A4
Bunker's Hl DVW CT17......38 A2
Bunkers Hill Av DVW CT17......38 A3
Bunkers Hill Rd DVW CT17......38 A3
Bunkley Meadow RASHW TN26......72 B4
Bunkley Ter RASHW TN26 *......72 B4
Burgess Cl DEAL CT14......22 B3
Burgess Gn DEAL CT14......8 A1
Burgoyne Hts RDV CT15......39 E2
Burlington House DVE/WH CT16 *......5 F5
Burrow Rd DEAL CT14......7 J2
Burton Cl FOLKN CT19......53 G5
Burton Rd KEN/WIL TN24......19 F3
Bushy Royds KEN/WIL TN24......43 H1
Buttermere Cl FOLKN CT19......6 B1
Butternut Copse ASH TN23......28 C5
Butterside Rd ASH TN23......43 G3
Butt Field Rd ASH TN23......28 C4
Bybrook Ct KEN/WIL TN24......19 E5
Bybrook Fld FOLK CT20......19 E5
Bybrook Rd KEN/WIL TN24......19 E5
Bybrook Wy FOLK CT20......67 E3
Byllan Rd DVW CT17......37 G1
Byron Crs DVE/WH CT16......22 B5

C

Cade Rd ASH TN23......29 E5
Caesar Av ASH TN23......42 D3
Caesar's Wy FOLKN CT19......53 D5
Calgary Crs FOLKN CT19......54 C4
Calgary Ter DVE/WH CT16 *......38 B1
Calland RASHE TN25......47 E2
Cambridge Gdns FOLK CT20......6 D4
Cambridge Rd DEAL CT14......11 H1
  DVW CT17......4 E7
Cambridge Ter FOLK CT20......7 G4
Camden Crs DVE/WH CT16......5 F6
Camden Ter KEN/WIL TN24......30 A5
Campbell Rd DEAL CT14......11 H1
Canada Cl FOLKN CT19......66 C1
Canada Ms DEAL CT14......11 G1
Canada Rd DEAL CT14......11 H1
Cannongate Av HYTHE CT21......65 F5
Cannongate Ci HYTHE CT21......65 G5
Cannongate Gdns HYTHE CT21......65 F4
Cannongate Rd HYTHE CT21......65 F4
Cannon St DEAL CT14......9 G4
Canons Gate Rd DVE/WH CT16......5 G4
Canon Woods Wy KEN/WIL TN24......19 H3
Canterbury Rd FOLKN CT19......7 G1
  KEN/WIL TN24......44 A1
  KEN/WIL TN24......3 H1
  RASHE TN25......14 A2
  RASHE TN25......7 E2
  RCANTW CT4......27 F5
  RDV CT15......20 A2
  RFOLK CT18......51 F1
  RFOLK CT18......7 F2
Capel Cl ASH TN23......2 B5
Capel Court Pk RFOLK CT18 *......55 F4
Capel St RFOLK CT18......55 F3
Capstan Rw DEAL CT14......9 H2
Carlsden Ct DVW CT17......38 A1
Carlton Rd ASH TN23......2 D2
  DEAL CT14......13 G1
Caroland Cl RASHE TN25......46 D2
Carter's Rd FOLK CT20......67 F2
Carter's Wd RASHE TN25......14 D2
Cassino Sq RDV CT15......39 E2
Castle Av DVE/WH CT16......4 D1
  HYTHE CT21......64 D4
Castle Bay FOLK CT20......66 C4
Castle Cl HYTHE CT21......64 D5
Castle Dr DVE/WH CT16......21 H2
Castle Hl FOLKN CT19......7 G1
Castle Hill Av FOLK CT20......6 C4
Castle Hill Rd DVE/WH CT16......5 C4
Castle Ms DEAL CT14......13 G1
Castlemount Rd DVE/WH CT16......4 D1
Castle Rd FOLK CT20......67 F4
  HYTHE CT21......64 D3
Castle St DVW CT17......5 F5
  KEN/WIL TN24......3 F5
Cauldham Cl RFOLK CT18......55 E3
Cauldham La RFOLK CT18......55 F2
Cavell Sq DEAL CT14......11 E1
Cavenagh Rd RDV CT15......25 F4
Caxton Cl TENT TN30......70 A5
Cecil Ct KEN/WIL TN24......3 F2
Cecil Rd DEAL CT14......11 H1
Cedar Cl ASH TN23......28 B4
The Cedars RASHE TN25......48 B4
Cedar Ter DVE/WH CT16 *......38 C1

Celtic Rd DEAL CT14 .... 11 E2
Cemetery La KEN/WIL TN24 .... 19 E5
Centre Rd DVW CT17 .... 4 C7
Centurion Wk ASH TN23 .... 43 F3
Chaffinch Dr ASH TN23 .... 43 G4
Chalcroft Rd FOLK CT20 .... 67 E5
Chalk Av TENT TN30 .... 70 D3
Chalk Cl FOLKN CT19 .... 53 G5
Chalk Hill Rd DEAL CT14 .... 13 G2
Chamberlain Rd DVW CT17 .... 38 A4
Chance Meadow RDV CT15 .... 23 F5
Channel Cl FOLKN CT19 .... 54 D5
Channel Lea DEAL CT14 .... 11 G3
Channel View Rd DVW CT17 .... 58 C1
Chapel La DEAL CT14 .... 10 B4
RCANTW CT4 .... 27 E1
RDV CT15 .... 20 D5
Chapel Pl DVW CT17 .... 4 E5
Chapel Rd DVE/WH CT16 .... 22 A1
Chapel St DEAL CT14 .... 9 H3
HYTHE CT21 .... 64 D5
Charles Crs FOLKN CT19 .... 53 E5
Charles Rd DEAL CT14 .... 9 F5
Charlotte St FOLK CT20 .... 7 C3
DEAL CT14 .... 9 F5
Charlton Av DVE/WH CT16 .... 4 C1
Charlton Cl KEN/WIL TN24 .... 30 C4
Charlton Gn DVE/WH CT16 .... 4 C1
Charminster ASH TN23 .... 42 C1
Chart Rd ASH TN23 .... 2 B2
ASH TN23 .... 28 B3
FOLKN CT19 .... 67 F1
Chater Cl ASH TN23 .... 28 A4
Chaucer Crs DVE/WH CT16 .... 38 B1
Chequers Pk RASHE TN25 .... 15 E3
Cheriton Court Rd FOLK CT20 .... 66 C1
Cheriton Gdns FOLK CT20 .... 6 D4
Cheriton High St RFOLK CT18 .... 66 B1
Cheriton Int FOLKN CT19 .... 66 C1
Cheriton Pl DEAL CT14 * 9 H5
FOLK CT20 .... 6 E5
Cheriton Rd FOLK CT20 .... 6 D4
FOLKN CT19 .... 67 F1
Cherrybrook Rd FOLK CT20 .... 66 D1
Cherry Garden La FOLK CT20 .... 67 G1
Cherry Garden Crs RASHE TN25 .... 15 F5
Cherry Garden La FOLKN CT19 .... 53 F5
RCANTW CT4 .... 27 H1
Cherry Gdns ASH TN23 .... 43 E2
Cherry Glebe RASHE TN25 .... 45 G4
Cherry La DEAL CT14 .... 10 B1
Cherry Tree Av DVW CT17 .... 4 A2
Cherrywood Ri RASHE TN25 .... 18 B5
Chester Rd RASHW TN26 .... 40 C2
Chestnut Cl ASH TN23 .... 28 C1
DVE/WH CT16 .... 22 A1
HYTHE CT21 .... 22 A1
TENT TN30 .... 70 D3
Chestnut La ASH TN23 .... 43 G3
Chestnut Rd DVW CT17 .... 38 B5
Chestnuts RASHE TN25 .... 46 D2
The Chestnuts RASHE TN25 * 46 B3
Chestnut Ter HYTHE CT21 * 75 E1
Chevalier Rd DVW CT17 .... 38 A5
Cheviot Wy KEN/WIL TN24 .... 19 E5
Chichester Cl ASH TN23 .... 43 E4
Chichester Rd FOLK CT20 .... 66 D1
Chilham Rd FOLKN CT19 .... 66 D1
Chiltern End KEN/WIL TN24 .... 2 F1
Chilton Av DVE/WH CT16 .... 37 E1
Chilton Wy DVW CT17 .... 37 G1
The Chimes KEN/WIL TN24 .... 3 F1
Chislett Cl RASHE TN25 .... 48 C2
Chisnall Rd DVW CT17 .... 21 D3
Christchurch Av ASH TN23 .... 2 E6
Christ Church Rd FOLK CT20 .... 6 C1
Christchurch Wy DVE/WH CT16 .... 38 B1
Christopher Bushell Wy
KEN/WIL TN24 .... 19 G5
Church Cliff DEAL CT14 .... 13 H1
Church Cl RASHE TN25 .... 45 G4
Church Fld RASHE TN25 .... 45 F5
Churchfield Wy RASHE TN25 .... 15 E2
Church Hts HYTHE CT21 * 75 E1
DVE/WH CT16 * 21 F4
RASHW TN26 .... 40 C2
RFOLK CT18 .... 35 G5
Churchill Av FOLKN CT19 .... 11 C2
Churchill Cl FOLKN CT19 .... 54 A4
FOLKN CT19 .... 54 A4
Churchill House Hts 24 D5
FOLKN CT19 * 38 B1
Churchill Rd DVW CT17 .... 58 A1
Churchill St DVW CT17 .... 4 C1
Church La DEAL CT14 .... 9 E4
DEAL CT14 .... 12 D2
RASHW TN26 .... 60 C4
RDV CT15 .... 20 A1
RDV CT15 .... 56 D3
Church Mdw DEAL CT14 .... 9 E4
Church Pth DEAL CT14 .... 9 E4
Church Rd ASH TN23 .... 3 C5
DVW CT17 .... 38 A5
FOLK CT20 .... 66 C1
HYTHE CT21 .... 65 E5
KEN/WIL TN24 .... 19 G3
KEN/WIL TN24 .... 44 D1
RASHE TN25 .... 15 G3
RFOLK CT18 .... 33 G2
TENT TN30 .... 70 B5
Church St DEAL CT14 .... 9 F2
DVE/WH CT16 .... 4 C5
FOLK CT20 .... 6 D3
RASHE TN25 .... 15 G2
Church Wk RCANTW CT4 * 27 H2
Churchyard ASH TN23 .... 3 D5
Cinque Ports Av HYTHE CT21 .... 75 F1
Citadel Crs DVW CT17 .... 58 A1
Citadel Rd DVW CT17 .... 58 C1
Clanwilliam Rd DEAL CT14 .... 9 H4
Claremont Rd DEAL CT14 .... 9 F4
DEAL CT14 .... 13 G1
FOLK CT20 .... 6 D4
Clarence Pl DEAL CT14 .... 9 F5
DVW CT17 .... 58 D2

Clarence Rd DEAL CT14 .... 11 H1
RFOLK CT18 .... 55 F2
Clarence St FOLK CT20 .... 7 G3
Clarendon Pl DVW CT17 .... 4 B6
Clarendon Rd DVW CT17 .... 4 C6
DVW CT17 .... 4 A6
Claridge Ms HYTHE CT21 * 65 E5
Clarke Crs KEN/WIL TN24 .... 19 G4
Clarke's Cl DEAL CT14 .... 8 D5
Claudius Gv ASH TN23 .... 42 D2
Claygate ASH TN23 .... 42 C2
Cleveland Cl DVE/WH CT16 .... 38 B3
Cleves Wy ASH TN23 .... 28 C4
Cliff Cl HYTHE CT21 .... 65 F4
Cliffe Rd DEAL CT14 .... 13 H1
Clifford Gdns DEAL CT14 .... 11 E2
Cliff Rd FOLK CT20 .... 67 G4
HYTHE CT21 .... 65 F4
Clifton Crs FOLK CT20 .... 6 B7
Clifton Gdns FOLK CT20 .... 6 D6
Clive Dennis Ct KEN/WIL TN24 .... 30 A3
Clockhouse ASH TN23 .... 3 A5
The Close ASH TN23 .... 28 C5
FOLKN CT19 .... 54 C4
HYTHE CT21 .... 64 D3
RASHE TN25 .... 15 E3
RDV CT15 .... 20 B1
Clouston Cl HYTHE CT21 .... 35 E4
Clynton Wy ASH TN23 .... 29 E5
Coach Dr RASHW TN26 .... 17 E2
Coach Rd RFOLK CT18 .... 34 C1
Coastguard Cots HYTHE CT21 * 65 F5
Cobay Cl HYTHE CT21 .... 65 F5
Cobbs Ms FOLK CT20 .... 6 D5
Cobden Rd HYTHE CT21 .... 75 F1
Cock La RASHW TN26 .... 72 B4
RCANTW CT4 .... H2
Coldblow DEAL CT14 .... 10 D5
Coldharbour La RASHE TN25 .... 15 F2
Coldred Hl RDV CT15 .... 20 B1
Colin's Wy HYTHE CT21 .... 66 A4
Collard Rd KEN/WIL TN24 .... 30 A5
Collards La RCANTW CT4 .... 27 F3
College Rd DEAL CT14 .... 9 H5
College Rw DVW CT17 * 38 B5
Collie Dr ASH TN23 .... 42 C2
Collingbourne ASH TN23 .... 42 C1
Collingwood Cl DEAL CT14 .... 11 G3
Collingwood Rd RDV CT15 .... 24 D2
Collingwood Rd East RDV CT15 .... 25 E1
Collison Pl TENT TN30 .... 71 E5
Colonel Stephens Wy TENT TN30 .... 70 B3
Colorado Cl DVE/WH CT16 .... 38 B3
Colton Crs DVE/WH CT16 .... 22 B5
Commercial Quay DVW CT17 .... 4 D7
Common La DVW CT17 .... 37 G1
The Conifers DEAL CT14 .... 11 E2
Coniston Rd FOLKN CT19 .... 54 C4
Conker Cl ASH TN23 .... 43 G4
Connaught Rd DVE/WH CT16 .... 4 D1
FOLK CT20 .... 6 A3
Constable's Rd DVE/WH CT16 .... 4 D1
Constantine Rd ASH TN23 .... 42 D2
Convent Ct RDV CT15 .... 56 E4
Coolinge La FOLK CT20 .... 67 F2
Coolinge Rd FOLK CT20 .... 6 F2
Coombe Cl DVW CT17 .... 38 A3
Coombe La TENT TN30 .... 70 B5
Coombe Rd DVW CT17 .... 37 F4
FOLKN CT19 .... 67 F1
Coombe Valley Rd DVW CT17 .... 38 A4
Coombe Wy FOLKN CT19 .... 54 A1
Coombe Wood La RFOLK CT18 .... 35 E5
Cooper's La RASHE TN25 .... 45 F5
Copperfield Cl KEN/WIL TN24 .... 19 E4
Copperwood ASH TN23 .... 19 E5
Coppin St DEAL CT14 .... 9 F2
The Copse ASH TN23 .... 28 C1
Copthall Gdns FOLK CT20 .... 7 F4
Cornbrook Rd HYTHE CT21 .... 74 B2
Corner Fld ASH TN23 .... 43 F2
Corner House Blds HYTHE CT21 * 64 D5
Cornes Cl KEN/WIL TN24 .... 30 C3
The Corniche FOLK CT20 .... 66 C4
Cornwallis Av FOLKN CT19 .... 6 A2
Cornwallis Cl FOLKN CT19 .... 6 A2
KEN/WIL TN24 .... 30 C5
Cornwall Rd DEAL CT14 .... 11 G1
Coronation Cots FOLKN CT19 * 6 D1
Coronation Dr ASH TN23 .... 28 A3
Corone Cl FOLKN CT19 .... 53 G5
Corunna Cl HYTHE CT21 .... 64 D5
Corunna Pl DVW CT17 .... 39 E1
Cotswold Cl FOLKN CT19 .... 53 G5
Coulter Rd ASH TN23 .... 43 E4
County Sq ASH TN23 * 3 F3
Court Ap FOLK CT20 .... 6 C5
Courtenay Rd DEAL CT14 .... 9 E5
Courtland Cl DEAL CT14 .... 22 A3
Cortland Dr DVE/WH CT16 .... 22 A3
Courtlands DEAL CT14 .... 13 H1
Courtlands DEAL CT14 .... 11 E2
Court Wurtin Beaver La
The Courtyard KEN/WIL TN24 .... 29 E5
Cowdray Rd DEAL CT14 .... 11 F1
Cowdray Sq DEAL CT14 .... 11 F1
Cowdrey Cl KEN/WIL TN24 .... 30 C5
Cowgate Hl DVW CT17 .... 4 B6
Cowgate La RFOLK CT18 .... 55 F3
Cow La DVW CT17 .... 38 A5
Cowper Rd DEAL CT14 .... 9 F4
DVW CT17 .... 37 G2
Coxhill Dr ASH TN23 .... 37 F1
Coxhill Gdns DVW CT17 .... 37 F1
Crabble Av DVW CT17 .... 38 A2
Crabble Cl DVW CT17 .... 37 H2
Crabble Hl DVW CT17 .... 38 A2
Crabble La DVW CT17 .... 37 H2
Crabble Mdw DVW CT17 .... 38 A2
Crabble Rd DVW CT17 .... 38 A2
Cradle Bridge Dr KEN/WIL TN24 .... 30 A2
Crafford St DVW CT17 .... 4 C4
Cranleigh Dr DVE/WH CT16 .... 22 A2
Cranleigh Gn FOLK CT20 .... 66 D2
Craythorne TENT TN30 .... 70 C5
Craythorne Cl TENT TN30 .... 66 B5
The Crescent FOLK CT20 .... 67 E4
KEN/WIL TN24 .... 44 B1

Cressfield ASH TN23 .... 25 E5
Crete Rd East RFOLK CT18 .... 54 A5
Crete Rd West RFOLK CT18 .... 54 A3
Creteway Cl RFOLK CT19 * 54 C4
Cricketers Cl RFOLK CT18 .... 35 E3
Cripps La RASHW TN26 .... 60 B1
Cripps' La RDV CT15 .... 24 D4
Crofters Cl HYTHE CT21 .... 74 C2
Croft La FOLK CT20 .... 67 F2
Crofton Cl KEN/WIL TN24 .... 30 C3
Croft Rd DEAL CT14 .... 9 F3
Croft Rd KEN/WIL TN24 .... 3 J4
Croft Road Flats KEN/WIL TN24 .... 3 J4
Croftwood ASH TN23 .... 42 B1
Cromwell Park Pl FOLK CT20 .... 66 D3
Crooked S Rd DEAL CT14 .... 9 E2
Crook's Court La RDV CT15 .... 56 B3
Cross Rd DEAL CT14 .... 11 E3
Cross Stile ASH TN23 .... 25 F3
Crosswall Quay DVW CT17 .... 58 D1
Crothall Hvn KEN/WIL TN24 .... 3 F2
Crowbridge Rd KEN/WIL TN24 .... 44 B1
Crownfield Rd ASH TN23 .... 2 A7
Crundale Cl ASH TN23 .... 42 A1
Cryol Rd ASH TN23 .... 28 D5
Cuckoo La ASH TN23 .... 42 A1
FOLKN CT19 .... 52 B2
Cudworth Rd KEN/WIL TN24 .... 29 H5
Cullens Hl RCANTW CT4 .... 27 G2
Culling's Hl RCANTW CT4 .... 27 H2
Curlew Rd RFOLK CT18 .... 55 E3
Curtis Rd TENT TN30 .... 70 C4
Curtis Wy DEAL CT14 .... 30 A5
Curzon Cl DEAL CT14 .... 11 G1
Curzon Rd DVW CT17 .... 4 A4
Custom House Quay DVW CT17 .... 58 D1
Cygnet Wy ASH TN23 .... 2 A5
Cylinder Rd HYTHE CT21 .... 64 D3
Cypress Av ASH TN23 .... 28 C2

D

Dale Wk KEN/WIL TN24 .... 19 E2
Dallas-Brett Crs FOLKN CT19 .... 54 C4
Dalmeny Ter HYTHE CT21 * 64 C5
Danemore TENT TN30 .... 70 C4
Danes Ct DVE/WH CT16 .... 38 C2
Danton La RFOLK CT18 .... 52 C3
Darby Pl FOLK CT20 .... 7 F3
Darby Rd FOLK CT20 .... 7 F3
Darlinghurst Rd FOLKN CT19 .... 53 E5
Darlington St FOLK CT20 .... 6 E3
Darnley Cl FOLK CT20 .... 67 F3
Darracott Cl DEAL CT14 .... 9 F4
Davis Av DEAL CT14 .... 9 F5
Dawson Rd FOLKN CT19 .... 7 F1
Deal Castle Rd DEAL CT14 .... 9 H4
Dean Md FOLKN CT19 .... 53 H5
Deanwood Rd DVW CT17 .... 37 G3
De Burgh Hl DVW CT17 .... 4 B2
De Burgh St DVW CT17 .... 4 B2
Deedes Cl HYTHE CT21 .... 65 E4
De Havilland Cl RFOLK CT18 .... 35 E5
Delane Rd DEAL CT14 .... 9 F5
Demozay Cl RFOLK CT18 .... 34 D5
Denbigh Dr ASH TN23 * 29 F4
Dencora Wy ASH TN23 .... 2 D5
The Dene HYTHE CT21 * 65 E5
RASHW TN26 .... 40 C2
Denmark St FOLKN CT19 .... 7 H1
Denmark Ter ASH TN23 * 3 G7
Dennes Mill La RASHE TN25 .... 14 D2
Denness Rd ASH TN23 .... 29 F5
Dennis Wy FOLKN CT19 .... 53 E5
Densole La RFOLK CT18 .... 34 D3
Densole La RFOLK CT18 .... 34 D1
Dental St HYTHE CT21 .... 65 E5
Dering Rd KEN/WIL TN24 .... 3 K4
Devon Av DEAL CT14 .... 11 G1
Deverton Rd FOLKN CT19 .... 7 F3
Devonshire Rd DVW CT17 .... 4 B6
Dexter Cl RASHE TN25 .... 19 E1
Deyley Wy ASH TN23 .... 28 A4
Diamond Cl FOLKN CT19 .... 53 F5
Diana Gdns DEAL CT14 .... 9 E4
Diddin Rd DEAL CT14 .... 12 C5
Dickson Rd DVW CT17 .... 4 B5
Dieu Stone La DVE/WH CT16 .... 5 F4
Digby Rd FOLK CT20 .... 67 G2
Dixwell Rd FOLK CT20 .... 67 G3
Dock Rd RDV DVE/WH CT16 .... 5 E4
Dodd's La DVE/WH CT16 .... 38 A1
Dog Kennel La RFOLK CT18 .... 32 C3
Dola Av DEAL CT14 .... 9 E4
Dolphin La DVE/WH CT16 .... 5 F5
Dolphin Pas DVE/WH CT16 .... 5 F5
Dolphins Rd FOLKN CT19 .... 54 A5
Dolphin St DEAL CT14 .... 9 F2
Dorset Gdns DEAL CT14 .... 11 G1
Douglas Av HYTHE CT21 .... 65 E5
Douglas Rd DEAL CT14 .... 11 E1
DVW CT17 .... 4 C3
Douro Cl FOLK CT20 .... 7 F1
Dour Side DVW CT17 .... 37 H1
Dour St DVE/WH CT16 .... 4 D5
Dove Cl ASH TN23 .... 2 D5
HYTHE CT21 .... 74 B2
Dovedale Ct KEN/WIL TN24 * 2 E1
Dove Lea Gdns DVW CT17 .... 4 C1
Dover Hl RFOLK CT18 .... 54 D5
Dover Pl ASH TN23 .... 3 J5
Dover Rd DEAL CT14 .... 11 E1
FOLK CT20 .... 7 G3
RDV CT15 .... 23 E5
Down Cl ASH TN23 .... 42 C2
Downhill Cl DVE/WH CT16 * 21 F3
Downland Cl RFOLK CT18 .... 34 D5
Downlands DEAL CT14 .... 13 F1
Downs Cl RFOLK CT18 .... 34 D5
Downside FOLKN CT19 .... 53 H5
RDV CT15 .... 25 E4
Downside DVE/WH CT16 .... 38 C3
Downs Rd DEAL CT14 .... 11 F1
FOLKN CT19 .... 54 A1
Downs Wy RASHE TN25 .... 48 A3

Dragonfly Wy RFOLK CT18 .... 2 B6
Drake Rd KEN/WIL TN24 .... 30 A5
Drew La DEAL CT14 .... 8 D5
Drop Redoubt Rd DVW CT17 .... 4 A6
The Drove DVE/WH CT16 .... 37 F1
Droveway Gdns RDV CT15 .... 25 E2
The Droveway RDV CT15 .... 25 E2
Drum La ASH TN23 .... 3 J5
Drum Major Dr DEAL CT14 .... 8 D5
Drury Rd TENT TN30 .... 70 B5
Dryden Rd DVW CT17 .... 4 A2
Duck La RASHW TN26 .... 72 B4
Duck St RCANTW CT4 .... 27 E1
Duckworth Ct KEN/WIL TN24 .... 3 J4
Dudley Rd FOLKN CT19 .... 6 E1
KEN/WIL TN24 .... 3 J4
Dukes Meadow RASHW TN26 .... 40 C2
Duke St DEAL CT14 .... 9 F2
Dunedin Dr RFOLK CT18 .... 34 D5
Dunkery Ri KEN/WIL TN24 .... 19 E5
Dunkirk Sq RDV CT15 .... 25 E1
Dunnett Rd FOLKN CT19 .... 53 H5
Dunnock Rd RASHW TN26 .... 2 D5
Durban Crs DVE/WH CT16 .... 22 B5
Durham Cl DVW CT17 .... 38 C2
Durham Hl DVW CT17 .... 4 B7
The Durlocks FOLKN CT19 .... 7 J3
Dyke Rd DEAL CT14 .... 9 F4
Dymchurch Rd HYTHE CT21 .... 74 A4

E

Ealham Cl KEN/WIL TN24 .... 30 C3
Earl's Av FOLK CT20 .... 6 E4
Earls Av KEN/WIL TN24 .... 30 C3
Earlsfield Rd HYTHE CT21 .... 74 C2
Earlsworth Rd KEN/WIL TN24 .... 44 D1
Eastbrook Pl DVE/WH CT16 * 5 F5
FOLKN CT19 .... 7 F2
East Cliff Gdns FOLKN CT19 .... 7 J2
East Cliff DVE/WH CT16 .... 4 D5
East Cliff Pas FOLKN CT19 .... 7 J3
East Cross TENT TN30 .... 70 C5
Eastern Arm North DVE/WH CT16 .... 5 F5
Eastern Av ASH TN23 .... 3 H5
Eastern Docks Rdt DVE/WH CT16 .... 5 F5
Eastern Gdns KEN/WIL TN24 .... 3 F1
Eastern Service Rd DVE/WH CT16 .... 5 F5
Eastfields FOLKN CT19 .... 7 F3
Eastgate Rd TENT TN30 .... 70 C4
East Langdon Rd RDV CT15 .... 9 F5
East Lodge Rd ASH TN23 .... 3 G4
Eastmead Av ASH TN23 .... 43 F4
East Mountain La RASHE TN25 .... 15 G4
East Rp FOLK CT20 .... 6 D5
East Rd FOLK CT21 .... 65 E5
Eastry Cl ASH TN23 .... 43 E4
East Stour Wy KEN/WIL TN24 .... 3 K5
TENT TN30 .... 70 C4
FOLKN CT19 .... 53 G5
East Weald Dr TENT TN30 .... 70 A5
East Well TENT TN30 * 71 F5
Eastwell Barn Ms TENT TN30 .... 71 E5
Eastwell Cl RASHW TN26 .... 40 C2
Eastwell Gra RASHE TN25 .... 40 C2
Eastwell Mdw TENT TN30 .... 71 E5
Eaton Rd DVW CT17 .... 4 D3
Eaves Rd DVW CT17 .... 58 C1
Eckford Cl RFOLK CT18 .... 35 E3
Edgar Rd DVW CT17 .... 4 A2
Edgehill Cl FOLK CT20 .... 66 D3
Edinburgh Rd KEN/WIL TN24 .... 3 K4
Edred Rd DVW CT17 .... 4 A2
Edward Rd DEAL CT14 .... 11 E2
FOLKN CT19 .... 7 F3
Edwards Rd DVE/WH CT16 .... 38 C2
Effingham Crs DVW CT17 .... 4 A6
Effingham St DVW CT17 .... 4 A6
Egerton Rd RFOLK CT18 .... 35 E3
Egerton Vis FOLKN CT19 * 7 G2
Eggringe ASH TN23 .... 42 A1
Elham Valley Wy HYTHE CT21 .... 64 A1
RCANTW CT4 .... 27 E4
RFOLK CT18 .... 55 E3
Elizabeth Carter Av DEAL CT14 .... 9 F5
Elizabeth Dr RFOLK CT18 .... 55 E3
Elizabeth Gdns FOLKN CT19 .... 7 F2
Elizabeth Rd DVW CT17 * 4 D1
Elizabeth St DVW CT17 .... 4 D1
Ellens Rd DEAL CT14 .... 11 E2
Ellingham Wy ASH TN23 .... 28 A4
Elm Ct HYTHE CT21 .... 65 E5
Elmfield TENT TN30 .... 70 B5
Elm Gdns HYTHE CT21 .... 74 B2
Elmhurst Cl RASHE TN25 .... 15 F5
Elm Rd FOLKN CT19 .... 7 G3
Elms Hl RDV CT15 .... 20 B1
Elmstead Pl FOLK CT20 .... 66 D2
Elms Vale Rd DVW CT17 .... 37 H4
DVW CT17 .... 58 A1
Elventon Cl FOLKN CT19 .... 53 H5
Elvington La RFOLK CT18 .... 23 F5
Elwick La ASH TN23 .... 3 F3
Elwick Rd ASH TN23 .... 3 F4
Enbrook Rd FOLK CT20 .... 66 D3
Enbrook Va FOLKN CT19 .... 66 D3
Encombe FOLK CT20 .... 66 D2
Enfield Rd DEAL CT14 .... 9 E4
Eric Rd DVW CT17 .... 58 C1
Erith St DVW CT17 .... 4 B2
Ernwell Rd FOLK CT20 .... 6 E4
Eshet Cl ASH TN23 .... 43 G4
Esplanade DVW CT17 .... 4 D6
Esplanade Quay DVW CT17 .... 4 D6
Essella Pk ASH TN23 .... 3 J4
Essella Rd ASH TN23 .... 3 J4
Essetford Rd ASH TN23 .... 42 D5
Etchden Rd RASHW TN26 .... 60 B3
Ethelbert Rd FOLK CT20 .... 6 D4
FOLKN CT19 .... 7 F3
Ethelburga Dr RFOLK CT18 .... 55 E3
Ettrick Ter HYTHE CT21 * 64 D5
Evans Rd KEN/WIL TN24 .... 30 A5
Evergreen Wy ASH TN23 .... 2 D5

y Rd HYTHE CT21 66 A4
y Wy FOLK CT20 57 F3
d DVE/WH CT16 38 H2
ge St DEAL CT14 9 D1
i FOLKN CT19 66 D1
r Ri KEN/WIL TN24 19 E5
ne Cl KEN/WIL TN24 19 F4

F

Cl FOLK CT20 66 D3
d DEAL CT14 8 D3
TW CT17 27 H1
d Ter RASHW TN26 72 B4
nt Rd HYTHE CT21 64 C4
w Dr ASH TN23 43 A1
w Gdns DEAL CT14 11 E2
ay Av HYTHE CT21 53 G5
rway DEAL CT14 9 G1
St DEAL CT14 9 G1
Wy ASH TN23 2
ld RASHW TN26 60 C1
n ASH TN23 2
r CT HYTHE CT21 65 F4
La DEAL CT14 9 H2
rs Rd HYTHE CT21 27 H1
mbe Wy DVE/WH CT16 22 B2
s Wk ASH TN23 43 F3
l RASHE TN25 18 B4
r St DEAL CT14 9 H2
ngoe Rd DVE/WH CT17 38 A1
na Dr ASH TN23 42 D3
ham Rd RASHE TN25 18 C1
t FOLKN CT19 67 E3
Gv HYTHE CT21 74 B2
Ms DEAL CT14 9 G5
KEN/WIL TN24 30 B3
FOLKN CT19 66 D1
FOLKN CT19 66 D1
s DEAL CT14 * 9 G1
l CT HYTHE CT21 7 H1
rket FOLKN CT19
onger's La DVE/WH CT16 * 1 F5
alter Ct DVE/WH CT16 * 22 B5
ays Ri DEAL CT14 8 D4
ers Fld RASHE TN25 28 D5
nd Rd RDV CT15 25 E1
ond RASHE TN25 25
ng Wy FOLKN CT19 54 B4
ers Wy DEAL CT14 9 E3
ell ASH TN23 42 B1
l DVE/WH CT16 38 B1
Horse La DVE/WH CT16 * 5 F5
Point Rd FOLK CT20 21 H5
Cl KEN/WIL TN24 30 C1
stone Rd DVW CT17 38 B5
/CT15 57 E3
Wood Wy HYTHE CT21 63 E3
Rd FOLK CT20 7 J2
Rd North FOLKN CT19 7 F4
Rd South FOLK CT20 7 F4
La DEAL CT14 2 A6
t FOLKN CT19 7 K1
s Sq DEAL CT14 11 F1
all Meadow ASH TN23 43 E3
t Av RASHE TN25 18 A4
ters Wy DEAL CT14 7 F4
field RASHW TN26 40 C2
Fld RDV CT15 56 A2
Hl RASHW TN26 40 D2
La ASH TN23 2 E3
t PDn DVE/WH CT16 22 A1
ove Rd DVE/WH CT16 22 A4
sters Pl ASH TN23 * 29 C4
n Cl TENT TN30 70 C4
orstal RASHE TN25 15 C2
Burgoyne Rd
E/WH CT16 5 C1
Rd HYTHE CT21 64 C4
Rd HYTHE CT21 42 C4
ll Gn ASH TN23 28 D5
r Cl FOLKN CT19 53 E5
r Rd KEN/WIL TN24 30 A4
r Wy DEAL CT14 9 F4
res Wy KEN/WIL TN24 18 C5
tains Cl KEN/WIL TN24 30 C3
I FOLKN CT19 32 D2
ove Gn KEN/WIL TN24 30 A3
ove Rd KEN/WIL TN24 30 A3
eaton Rd HYTHE CT21 64 C5
e Rd DVE/WH CT16 22 A4
cis Rd ASH TN23 29 F4
k Edinger Cl KEN/WIL TN24 19 F5
hy La RASHW TN26 11 E1
rick Rd DEAL CT14 11 E1
reedown RDV CT15 25 E1
nens Wy DEAL CT14 11 F1
antle Rd FOLK CT20 67
field La HYTHE CT21 64 A1
I Wy DVW CT17 38 A1
an Wy KEN/WIL TN24 19 E2
Rd DVE/WH CT16 4 C1
enden Ct ASH TN23 42 D2
La DEAL CT14 9 D2
st Rd DVE/WH CT16 22 B4
rt Rd FOLKN CT19 53 F1
er Av FOLK CT20 66 B2

G

borough Cl FOLKN CT19 53 C5
way Dr RASHE TN25 19 E1
n Dr KEN/WIL TN24 19 G3
n Rd FOLKN CT19 19 E2

Garton Wy ASH TN23 28 A5
Gasworks La ASH TN23 2 C5
Gate La RCANTW CT4 26 C2
The Gateway DVE/WH CT16 5 F5
Gaunt's Cl DEAL CT14 9 E5
Geddes Cl RFOLK CT18 53 H4
George Gurr Crs FOLKN CT19 53 F1
George St ASH TN23 7 G5
George St ASH TN23 3 F6
DEAL CT14 9 H2
DVW CT17 4 A1
George Williams Wy
KEN/WIL TN24 19 G4
Geraldine Rd FOLKN CT19 67 F1
Gibraltar La RFOLK CT18 53 F1
Gibraltar Sq RDV CT15 39 E1
Gilbert Rd DEAL CT14 3 F3
Gilford Rd DEAL CT14 9 F5
Gilford Rd HYTHE CT21 64 C4
Gill La RASHW TN26 72 D1
Gillman Cl RFOLK CT18 34 C5
Glack Rd DEAL CT14 8 D3
The Glade DEAL CT14 7 G1
Gladstone Rd DEAL CT14 7 G1
FOLKN CT19
KEN/WIL TN24 44 A1
Glebe Cl RDV CT15 39
Glebelands RASHE TN25 45 G2
Glebe Wy KEN/WIL TN24 19 F2
Glenfield Rd DVE/WH CT16 38 B1
Glen Gv DVW CT17 4 A5
Glen Rd DEAL CT14 9 G1
Glenwood Ter TENT TN30 * 70 C1
Glenwood Cl TENT TN30 70 C1
Gloster Cl RFOLK CT18 53 H1
Gloster Ropewalk
DVW CT17 58 C2
Gloster Ter FOLK CT20 * 66 D5
Gloster Wy DVW CT17 58 C2
Gloucester Pl FOLK CT20 7 H4
Glover Rd KEN/WIL TN24 30 A3
Goat Lees La RASHE TN25 19 F2
Godfrey Wk ASH TN23 3
Godinton La ASH TN23 2 D3
Godinton Rd ASH TN23 2 D3
Godinton Wy ASH TN23 2 D3
Godwin Rd DVE/WH CT16 5 H3
Godwyne Cl DVE/WH CT16 * 4 E3
Godwyne Ct DVE/WH CT16 * 4 E3
Godwyne Rd DVE/WH CT16 4 E3
Godwyn Gdns FOLK CT20 67 G3
Godwyn Rd DEAL CT14 9 G5
FOLK CT20 67 G3
Golden Sq TENT TN30 70 C4
Golden St DEAL CT14 9 H2
Goldsmith Ct TENT TN30 70 C4
Golf Rd DEAL CT14 9 G1
Golf Road Pl DEAL CT14 9 G1
Goodcheap La RASHE TN25 31 F1
Goodfellow Wy DVE/WH CT16 22 A5
Gordon Cl KEN/WIL TN24 3 K3
Gordon Rd FOLK CT20 66 D1
Goschen Rd DVW CT17 38 B4
Goteley Mere KEN/WIL TN24 19 F2
Gothic Cl DEAL CT14 11 F3
Gough Rd FOLK CT20 67 E4
Grace Hl FOLK CT20 7 H4
Grace Meadow ASH TN23 22 A2
Grace Taylor Ms FOLKN CT19 * 11 F1
Grams Rd DEAL CT14 11 H1
Gramary Court Rd RASHE TN25 47 G3
Grange Crs TENT TN30 70 B4
Grange Rd DEAL CT14 9 F1
FOLKN CT19 67 E1
HYTHE CT21 67
TENT TN30 70 A1
Grantham Av DEAL CT14 9 A1
Grantley Cl ASH TN23 29 E5
Granville Pde FOLK CT20 7 H4
Granville Rd DEAL CT14 11 C2
RDV CT15 25 H4
Granville Rd East FOLK CT20 67 E4
Granville St DEAL CT14 9 H4
DVE/WH CT16 4 B5
Grasmere Gdns FOLKN CT19 53 H5
Grasmere Rd KEN/WIL TN24 19 G5
Gravel La RDV CT15 56 B3
Gravelly Flds ASH TN23 28 C4
Gravel Wk KEN/WIL TN24 30
Gray Cl RFOLK CT18 35 F4
Graylen Cl DEAL CT14 9 C2
Great Conduit St HYTHE CT21 * 65 F5
Great Fishers ASH TN23 28 A5
Grebe Cl RFOLK CT18 34 C5
Grebe Crs HYTHE CT21 74 A2
Greenacre Dr DEAL CT14 11 G3
Greenbank KEN/WIL TN24 19 G3
Greenbanks RFOLK CT18 35 E5
Green Cl RFOLK CT18 35 E5
Green Ct FOLKN CT19 42 B1
Greencroft ASH TN23 42 B1
Greenfield Rd FOLKN CT19 42 B1
Greenfields RASHE TN25 48 C2
Green Fields La ASH TN23 42
Green Hedges TENT TN30 70 C2
Green La ASH TN23 42 C2
DEAL CT14 11 G3
DVE/WH CT16 21 E5
FOLKN CT19 42 C2
HYTHE CT21 64 A1
RDV CT15 24 D1
RFOLK CT18 35 E5
Green Lane Av HYTHE CT21 64 B5
Greensand Wy RASHW TN26 16 D1
Greensland Wy ASH TN23 42 A1
RASHW TN26 17 G3
The Green RASHE TN25 15 G2
RASHE TN25 15 G4
Grenadier Wy ASH TN23 28 A4
Greyhound Cha ASH TN23 28 B4
Grey Willow Gdns ASH TN23 28 B4
Grice Cl RFOLK CT18 28 A4
Griffin Cl ASH TN23 9 H2
Griffin St DEAL CT14 28 A4
Grimston Av FOLK CT20 6 A5
Grimston Gdns FOLK CT20 6 A5
Grosvenor Rd KEN/WIL TN24 11 H1
Grove Rd DEAL CT14 11 H1
FOLK CT20 7 G3

The Grove DEAL CT14 9 G3
DVE/WH CT16 4 C3
KEN/WIL TN24 19 G3
Guernsey Wy KEN/WIL TN24 19 E2
Guildhall St FOLK CT20 7 G3
Guildhall St North FOLKN CT19 6 E3
Guilford Av DVE/WH CT16 22 A5
Gurling Rd RDV CT15 24 D1
Guthrie Gdns DVW CT17 37 G1

H

Hackfield ASH TN23 2 B6
Hadrian Gdns ASH TN23 42 D2
Haffenden Rd TENT TN30 70 B3
Hales Cl TENT TN30 70 C3
Hall Av KEN/WIL TN24 44 B1
Hall Crs DEAL CT14 8 D1
Halliday Ct HYTHE CT21 * 64 C3
Halliday Dr DEAL CT14 11 G1
Halstatt Rd DEAL CT14 11 E1
Halstow Wy ASH TN23 28 D4
The Halt RCANTW CT4 27 H2
Hamilton Rd DEAL CT14 9 F1
DVW CT17 38 A4
KEN/WIL TN24 43 H1
Hammond's Rd FOLK CT20 67 E2
Hampden La ASH TN23 43 E5
Hampden Ms ASH TN23 43 E5
Hampden Rd ASH TN23 43 E5
Hampstreet Rd RASHW TN26 72 C4
Hampton V HYTHE CT21 66 A3
Hancocks Fld DEAL CT14 12 B2
Hangman's La DEAL CT14 12 B2
RDV CT15 23 C3
Hanover Cl ASH TN23 2 B4
DEAL CT14 11 H2
Harbour Approach Rd FOLK CT20 7 H4
Harbour St FOLK CT20 7 H4
Harbour View Rd DVE/WH CT16 38 B4
Harbour Wy FOLK CT20 7 H4
Harcourt Rd FOLKN CT19 53 F5
Hardinge Rd KEN/WIL TN24 58 B1
Hardwicke Rd DVW CT17 67 G3
Hardwick Rd FOLK CT20 67 G3
Hardy Cl KEN/WIL TN24 30 C5
Hardy Rd RDV CT15 24 C2
Harman Av HYTHE CT21 62 D4
Harold Rd DEAL CT14 9 G1
Harold's Rd DVE/WH CT16 4 E5
Harper Rd ASH TN23 2 B4
Harpswood La HYTHE CT21 64 C4
Harriot Cl FOLKN CT19 53 H5
Harrow Wy FOLKN CT19 53 H5
Harry Pay Cl KEN/WIL TN24 19 G5
Hart Cl RFOLK CT18 34 C5
Harvest Wy ASH TN23 28 B5
RFOLK CT18 35 E5
Harvey Av DEAL CT14 11 C1
Harvey Pl FOLK CT20 7 G3
Harvey Rd KEN/WIL TN24 30 B2
Harvey St FOLK CT20 7 G3
Harville Rd RASHE TN25 14 C2
Hasborough Rd FOLKN CT19 7 H4
Haskard Cl RFOLK CT18 34 C5
Havelock Rd DEAL CT14 11 C1
Haven Dr RFOLK CT18 34 C5
The Haven DEAL CT14 * 13 H1
HYTHE CT21 74 A2
Haventhorpe KEN/WIL TN24 19 G5
Hawkesbury St DVW CT17 58 C1
Hawkins Rd FOLKN CT19 66 B1
Hawksdown DEAL CT14 11 H4
Hawksdown Rd DEAL CT14 11 H4
Hawkshill Rd DEAL CT14 11 H4
Hawks Wy ASH TN23 28 C5
Hawthorn Cl DVW CT17 37 G2
HYTHE CT21 * 74 A2
Hawthorn Rd ASH TN23 43 F3
Haymakers La ASH TN23 28 A5
Hayton Rd RASHE TN25 49 E3
Haywain Cl ASH TN23 42 C2
Hayward Cl DEAL CT14 9 E5
Hazeldown Cl DVW CT17 37 G2
Hazel Hts RASHE TN25 45
Heartwood Dr ASH TN23 28 C1
Heather Dr TENT TN30 70 C3
Heathfield Av DVE/WH CT16 38 B2
Heathfield Rd KEN/WIL TN24 30 B5
Hedgerows ASH TN23 28 B5
Hedgers Wy ASH TN23 42 B3
Heights Ter DVW CT17 58 C1
Helena Corniche FOLK CT20 66 C4
Helena Rd RFOLK CT18 55 C2
Hempsted St ASH TN23 2 D3
Hengest Rd DEAL CT14 9 F1
Henley Flds TENT TN30 70 B3
Henley Mdw TENT TN30 70 B2
Henwood ASH TN23 3
Herbert Rd KEN/WIL TN24 43 H1
Herbert Street DVW CT17 * 4 A1
Herdson Rd FOLK CT20 67 G2
Hereford Cl ASH TN23 19 E2
Heritage Gdns DVE/WH CT16 5 F3
Heritage Rd FOLK CT20 7 F1
Hermitage Ct HYTHE CT21 64 D5
Heron Forstal Av RFOLK CT18 35 E5
Herons Wy HYTHE CT21 74 A2
Heron Wk ASH TN23 28 C4
Herschell Rd East DEAL CT14 11 C1
Herschell Rd West DEAL CT14 11 C1
Herschell Sq DEAL CT14 11 C1
Hestia Wy ASH TN23 42 C2
Hewitt Rd DVE/WH CT16 4 D1
Hewitts Pl KEN/WIL TN24 30 C5
Hextable Cl ASH TN23 42 C2
Heyford Cl RFOLK CT18 35 E5
High Bury La TENT TN30 70 B5
Highfield Cl HYTHE CT21 64 C3
Highfield La RASHE TN25 45 G2
Highfield Rd FOLKN CT19 53 H5
Highland Cl FOLK CT20 67 G3
High Meadow DVW CT17 4 A5
High Rdg ASH TN23 28 A5
Highridge HYTHE CT21 66 A4

High St DEAL CT14 9 H2
DVE/WH CT16 4 C3
DVE/WH CT16 21 F4
HYTHE CT21 65 E5
KEN/WIL TN24 3 F5
RASHE TN25 15 E2
RCANTW CT4 27 H1
RDV CT15 24 D1
RFOLK CT18 32 D3
TENT TN30 70 B5
High Trees Cl KEN/WIL TN24 30 C3
Highview Pk RFOLK CT18 55 E4
Hillbrow La ASH TN23 2 A6
Hillbrow Rd ASH TN23 2 C7
Hillcrest La ASH TN23 2 C7
Hillcrest Gdns DEAL CT14 19 G3
Hillcrest Rd DEAL CT14 13 G3
HYTHE CT21 64 D3
Hill La RFOLK CT18 52 B3
Hill Ri RASHE TN25 18 A4
Hill Rd FOLKN CT19 53 G5
Hillside DEAL CT14 67 E4
Hillside Rd DVW CT17 38 A2
Hillside St HYTHE CT21 64 D5
Hill Vw KEN/WIL TN24 3 F3
Hillyfield Rd ASH TN23 2 C7
Hillyfields ASH TN23 2 C6
Hillyfields Rd ASH TN23 2 B5
Hilton Rd ASH TN23 2 B5
Hinxhill Rd KEN/WIL TN24 31 E4
Hirst Ct DVW CT17 22 B5
Hoads Wood Gdns
RASHE TN25 18 A3
Hobart Crs DVE/WH CT16 38 B3
Hogben Cl RFOLK CT18 32 D2
Hog Gn RCANTW CT4 42 C1
Holdenhurst ASH TN23 42 C1
Hollands Av FOLKN CT19 54 D5
Hollington Pl KEN/WIL TN24 3 F2
Hollow Wood Rd DVW CT17 37 G4
Holly Cl FOLKN CT19 54 C5
HYTHE CT21 * 65 F4
Holly Mdw ASH TN23 28 B1
Holmesdale Ter DEAL CT14 7 F5
Holmestone Rd DVW CT17 37 G3
Holmlea Cl KEN/WIL TN24 30 A3
Holmwood Rd ASH TN23 28 A4
Holt Cl ASH TN23 28 A4
Holywell Av FOLKN CT19 54 A4
Homefield Av DEAL CT14 9 A4
Homefield Rw DEAL CT14 * 48 B3
Homelands Cl RASHE TN25 48 B3
Homestead ASH TN23 28 B4
Homestead Ct DEAL CT14 9 A4
Homewood Rd TENT TN30 70 C3
Honeywood Cl DVE/WH CT16 22 A3
Honeywood Pkwy
DVE/WH CT16 22 B4
Honeywood Rd DVE/WH CT16 22 B4
Honner Cl RFOLK CT18 53 F1
Hook Cl FOLK CT20 67 F2
Hope Rd DEAL CT14 9 H4
Hoppers Wy ASH TN23 28 B4
Hornash La RASHW TN26 60 D2
Hornbeam Cl ASH TN23 2 A2
Horn St HYTHE CT21 66 B4
Horsa Rd DEAL CT14 9 H1
Horsley Cl RFOLK CT18 53 G1
Hospital Hl HYTHE CT21 66 B4
Hotel Rd RFOLK CT18 25 F4
Hougham Court La RDV CT15 56 C4
House Fld KEN/WIL TN24 30 B3
House Meadow ASH TN23 28 B4
Hoxton Cl ASH TN23 28 B4
Hudson Cl DVE/WH CT16 38 B1
Hunt Cl RFOLK CT18 34 D5
Hunter Av KEN/WIL TN24 30 A4
Hunter Cl KEN/WIL TN24 30 A4
Hunter Rd KEN/WIL TN24 30 A4
Hunters Bank RCANTW CT4 27 G2
Hunters Wk DEAL CT14 9 E5
Huron Ter DVE/WH CT16 * 38 B1
Hurst Rd KEN/WIL TN24 18 D2
Hythe Cl FOLK CT20 67 F2
Hythe Rd HYTHE CT21 63 G3
KEN/WIL TN24 3 K4
RASHE TN25 45 H2
Hyton Dr DEAL CT14 9 F3

I

Ian's Wk HYTHE CT21 66 A4
Ilex Rd FOLKN CT19 67 F1
Imperial Wy ASH TN23 28 A5
Ingledon Park Rd TENT TN30 70 C3
Ingles La FOLK CT20 6 E4
Ingles Rd FOLK CT20 6 C5
Ingoldsby Rd FOLKN CT19 54 C5
Ingram Cl RFOLK CT18 53 F1
Invicta Rd FOLKN CT19 66 B1
Inward Car Lanes DVE/WH CT16 39 G4
Isis Cl HYTHE CT21 51 E4
Ivy Cl RFOLK CT18 53 F1
Ivy Wy FOLKN CT19 54 C5

J

Jacksons La TENT TN30 70 B5
Jacobs Oak KEN/WIL TN24 43 H1
James Allchin Gdns
KEN/WIL TN24 19 H5
James Cl RFOLK CT18 53 D2
James Hall Gdns DEAL CT14 11 C1
James Haney Dr KEN/WIL TN24 19 H4
James St ASH TN23 2 D3
FOLKN CT19 7 F2
Jarman's Fld RASHE TN25 15 F2
Jarvis Dr KEN/WIL TN24 30 C5
Jarvis Pl TENT TN30 30 A1
Jarvist Pl DEAL CT14 13 H1
Jefferson Cl DVW CT17 2 B5
Jellicoe Cl KEN/WIL TN24 30 C5
Jemmett La RASHE TN25 45 E3

Jemmett Rd ASH TN23 2 D7
Jersey Cl KEN/WIL TN24 19 E1
Jesmond St FOLKN CT19 6 E2
Johannesburg Rd DVE/WH CT16 22 C5
John Badger Cl KEN/WIL TN24 19 G4
John Dutton Wy KEN/WIL TN24 19 G5
John Newington Cl
KEN/WIL TN24 19 G4
Johnson Cl KEN/WIL TN24 30 C5
John Tapping Cl DEAL CT14 11 F3
Jointon Rd FOLK CT20 6 B5
Joyes Cl DVE/WH CT16 22 A2
FOLKN CT19 54 C5
Joyes Rd DVE/WH CT16 22 A2
FOLKN CT19 54 C5
Jubilee Cl HYTHE CT21 74 B2
Jubilee Dr DEAL CT14 11 H1
Jubilee Wy DVE/WH CT16 5 J4
Julian Rd FOLKN CT19 6 B3
Julien Pl KEN/WIL TN24 30 C4
Juniper Cl ASH TN23 28 C2
Jupiter La ASH TN23 42 C2

K

Kavelin Wy KEN/WIL TN24 30 A1
Kearsney Abbey Vls
DVE/WH CT16 * 21 F5
Kearsney Ct DVE/WH CT16 21 E5
Keddow's Cl HYTHE CT21 74 B2
Kedleston Rd DVE/WH CT16 22 C4
Kelvedon Rd DEAL CT14 11 G2
Kempes Pl RASHE TN25 * 15 E2
Kenbrook KEN/WIL TN24 19 E2
Kenilworth Cl RDV CT15 25 E4
Kennedy Dr DEAL CT14 11 F2
Kennett Dr DEAL CT14 11 E2
Kennett La RASHE TN25 49 E3
Kennington Pl KEN/WIL TN24 19 F2
Kennington Rd KEN/WIL TN24 30 C2
Kent Av KEN/WIL TN24 2 E2
Kent Rd FOLKN CT19 53 E5
Kestrel Cl ASH TN23 43 G4
Kettle Dr RFOLK CT18 35 E4
Keyes Cl DVE/WH CT16 22 A4
Keyes Pl FOLKN CT19 54 C5
The Keys RFOLK CT18 35 F4
Khartoum Sq DVE/WH CT16 22 A3
Kilndown Cl ASH TN23 42 C1
Kiln Fld TENT TN30 70 D5
Kiln La RASHW TN26 41 E3
Kimberley Cl DVE/WH CT16 38 C1
King Edward Rd DEAL CT14 9 G1
Kingfisher Av HYTHE CT21 74 B2
Kingfisher Cl KEN/WIL TN24 30 C5
King Lear's Wy DVW CT17 * 58 B2
Kings Av ASH TN23 2 C3
Kings Cha KEN/WIL TN24 30 C2
King's Cl DEAL CT14 13 G2
Kingsdown Hl DEAL CT14 13 G3
Kingsdown Pk DEAL CT14 * 13 H2
Kingsdown Rd DEAL CT14 11 H4
RDV CT15 24 D3
Kingsford St RASHE TN25 45 F1
Kingsford Ter ASH TN23 * 43 E1
Kingsland Gdns DEAL CT14 11 F4
Kingsland La RASHE TN25 18 B2
Kingsmead FOLKN CT19 53 H4
Kings Meadow RASHE TN25 19 G2
Kingsnorth Gdns FOLK CT20 6 B4
Kingsnorth Rd ASH TN23 43 E1
Kings Pde KEN/WIL TN24 * 3 F3
King's Prospect KEN/WIL TN24 43 H1
Kings Rd DVW CT17 38 A5
FOLK CT20 66 D1
Kings Ropewalk DVW CT17 58 B2
Kingston Cl DVW CT17 37 H1
King St DEAL CT14 11 H1
DVE/WH CT16 4 E5
Kingswood KEN/WIL TN24 19 F4
Kingswood Vls DVW CT17 * 38 A2
Kipling Rd ASH TN23 2 E3
Kipping Cl RFOLK CT18 34 D5
Kirk Vw ASH TN23 28 A5
Kirton Cl RFOLK CT18 34 C5
Kitchener Rd DVW CT17 38 A5
Kitchener Sq FOLKN CT19 54 C4
Kither Rd ASH TN23 29 E5
Knatchbull Wy RASHE TN25 47 E2
Knight's Rd DVE/WH CT16 5 G3
Knights Templars DVW CT17 4 C7
Knights Wy DVE/WH CT16 38 A1
Knock Rd ASH TN23 29 E5
Knockwood Rd TENT TN30 70 D3
Knoll La ASH TN23 28 C5
Knoll Pl DEAL CT14 11 G3
Knott Crs KEN/WIL TN24 30 C5
Knotts La RDV CT15 24 D4
Kohima Pl RDV CT15 39 F2
Kymbeline Ct DEAL CT14 9 F5

L

Laburnum Cl DVE/WH CT16 21 G5
Lachlan Wy FOLK CT20 67 F4
Lacton Oast KEN/WIL TN24 30 D4
Lacton Wy KEN/WIL TN24 30 C4
Lady Garne Rd RDV CT15 56 B2
Ladywell DVE/WH CT16 4 D3
Lakemead ASH TN23 28 C4
Lakeside ASH TN23 * 28 C3
Lambton Rd DVW CT17 38 A3
Lancaster Av RFOLK CT18 55 F2
Lancaster Cl RASHW TN26 72 B3
Lancaster Rd DVW CT17 4 D5
Lancelot Cl DEAL CT14 11 E1
Landbury Wk RASHE TN25 18 B5
The Lane RDV CT15 23 F3
Lanfranc Rd DEAL CT14 9 G1
Langdale ASH TN23 28 C4
Langdon Cl RDV CT15 24 D5
Langdon Rd FOLKN CT19 52 D5
Langholm Rd ASH TN23 29 E5
Langhorne Gdns FOLK CT20 6 D6
Langney Dr ASH TN23 42 B1
Langton Rd DEAL CT14 9 G1
Lapwing Cl RFOLK CT18 53 G1
Lapwing Dr ASH TN23 43 H4
Larch Wk KEN/WIL TN24 19 E3
Lascelles Rd DVW CT17 58 A1
La-Tene DEAL CT14 11 F2
Laurel Cl FOLK CT20 67 E1
Laureston Pl DVE/WH CT16 5 F3
Lawn Cl TENT TN30 70 A5
Lawn Rd DEAL CT14 11 G3
Lawrence Cl FOLKN CT19 67 F1
Lawrence Ct FOLKN CT19 7 H1
Lea Cl HYTHE CT21 64 D3
Leacon Rd ASH TN23 2 A5
Leafield RASHE TN25 48 B3
Leaside Cots HYTHE CT21 * 64 D4
Leas Rd DEAL CT14 9 F4
The Leas DEAL CT14 13 H4
FOLK CT20 6 C7
Leaveland Cl ASH TN23 42 D1
The Lees Cl RASHE TN25 46 D2
Lees Rd KEN/WIL TN24 30 C3
Leighton Rd DVE/WH CT16 4 B1
Leivers Rd DEAL CT14 11 E1
Lenacre Av DVE/WH CT16 21 H2
Lenacre La DVE/WH CT16 21 H1
Lennard Rd FOLK CT20 7 H3
Le Roux Cl RFOLK CT18 34 C5
Leslie Crs TENT TN30 70 C2
Lewis Ct ASH TN23 * 28 D5
Lewisham Rd DVW CT17 37 G1
Leyburne Rd DVE/WH CT16 4 E2
Lilac Ct ASH TN23 28 C1
Lilyvale Rd RASHE TN25 47 F3
Lime Cl ASH TN23 2 A2
Limekiln Rbt DVW CT17 58 C1
Limes Cl TENT TN30 70 D4
Limes Rd DVE/WH CT16 4 C1
FOLKN CT19 67 F1
The Limes ASH TN23 42 D2
The Linces DVE/WH CT16 22 B5
Linden Crs FOLKN CT19 7 F1
Linden Dr RCANTW CT4 27 H1
Linden Rd KEN/WIL TN24 3 J4
Links Rd DEAL CT14 9 G1
Linksway FOLKN CT19 53 G5
Linksway Cl FOLKN CT19 53 H5
Lister Cl DEAL CT14 9 G4
DVW CT17 4 A1
Lister Wy FOLK CT20 * 67 F4
Little Av DEAL CT14 8 D5
Littlebrook Cl ASH TN23 2 C1
Little Brook Rd ASH TN23 2 C1
Little Chequers RASHE TN25 15 E2
Little Knoll ASH TN23 2 B7
Little Md FOLKN CT19 53 G5
Little Tilden Gill TENT TN30 70 D5
Liverpool Rd DEAL CT14 11 G4
Lockholt Cl ASH TN23 28 C1
Lodge Wood Dr RASHE TN25 18 A4
London Rd DEAL CT14 8 C3
DVE/WH CT16 21 G5
DVW CT17 4 B1
DVW CT17 21 G5
HYTHE CT21 64 B4
RDV CT15 20 D3
London Road Temple Ewell
DVE/WH CT16 21 E4
London St FOLK CT20 7 H3
Lonefield RASHW TN26 60 D1
Longacre Rd ASH TN23 28 B5
Longage Hl RCANTW CT4 26 C4
The Long Barrow KEN/WIL TN24 44 A2
Long Beech ASH TN23 28 C3
Longbridge KEN/WIL TN24 30 D3
Longbridge Ter HYTHE CT21 * 75 E1
Longfield TENT TN30 70 B5
Longfield Rd DVW CT17 58 B1
Longford Ter FOLK CT20 7 F6
Longford Wy FOLK CT20 6 E6
Long Length RASHW TN26 42 B4
Lookers La HYTHE CT21 64 D4
Lord Warden Av DEAL CT14 11 H2
Lord Warden Sq DVW CT17 58 D2
Loudon Ct ASH TN23 28 C1
Loudon Wy ASH TN23 17 H5
Lourdse Manor Cl RASHE TN25 48 B3
Lovelace Ct RASHW TN26 40 B2
Lower Blackhouse Hl HYTHE CT21 65 F5
Lower Denmark Rd ASH TN23 3 G7
Lower Mill La DEAL CT14 9 G4
Lower Rd DVE/WH CT16 21 F4
Lower Rd East DVE/WH CT16 39 H4
Lower Sandgate Rd FOLK CT20 7 F6
Lower Vicarage Rd KEN/WIL TN24 19 E2
Lowslip Hl RDV CT15 56 B2
Lowther Rd DVW CT17 4 A3
Loxford Ldg FOLK CT20 * 66 D5
Loxwood Cl DVE/WH CT16 22 B2
Lucerne La RDV CT15 12 A5
Lucilla Av ASH TN23 42 D2
Luckhurst Rd DVW CT17 37 G1
KEN/WIL TN24 30 C5
Lucknow Cl RDV CT15 39 F1
Lucy Av FOLKN CT19 53 G5
Lucy's Hl HYTHE CT21 64 D5
Luddenham Cl ASH TN23 42 D1
Lukes Cl DVW CT17 38 A3
Lydia Rd DEAL CT14 11 E2
Lyell Cl HYTHE CT21 75 E1
Lympne Hl HYTHE CT21 63 E5
Lyndhurst Rd DVW CT17 37 G2
Lyndon Wy RFOLK CT18 33 E2
Lynsted Cl ASH TN23 42 D1
Lynton Rd HYTHE CT21 75 G1
Lysander Wk RFOLK CT18 34 D5

M

Mabledon Av KEN/WIL TN24 3 K5
Macdonald Rd DVW CT17 38 A3
Mace La KEN/WIL TN24 3 H3
Mackenzie Dr FOLK CT20 67 E2
Mackenzie Ter DVE/WH CT16 * 38 B1
Magazine Rd KEN/WIL TN24 3 F2
Magdala Rd DVW CT17 4 A1
Magness Rd DEAL CT14 11 E2
Magpie Hall Rd RASHW TN26 42 B5
Magpie La RCANTW CT4 26 D3
Maidstone Rd KEN/WIL TN24 2 D2
RASHE TN25 18 B4
Maine Cl DVE/WH CT16 38 B1
Maison Dieu Rd DVE/WH CT16 4 D3
Malcolm Sargent Rd ASH TN23 43 F1
Mallards KEN/WIL TN24 29 H5
Malmains Rd DVW CT17 38 A5
Malmeady Ct DEAL CT14 * 11 E3
Malthouse Hl HYTHE CT21 64 D5
Malt House La TENT TN30 70 B5
The Maltings DEAL CT14 11 F4
Malvern Meadow DVE/WH CT16 21 G4
Malvern Rd DVE/WH CT16 21 G4
DVW CT17 4 B5
KEN/WIL TN24 18 D5
Mangers La DVE/WH CT16 38 A2
Mangers Pl DVE/WH CT16 38 A1
Manley Cl DVE/WH CT16 22 A2
Mannering Cl DVW CT17 37 H1
Manor Av DEAL CT14 9 F5
Manor Cl DEAL CT14 9 E5
Manor Farm Cl HYTHE CT21 62 D3
Manorfield ASH TN23 28 C4
Manor House Dr ASH TN23 43 G3
Manor Leaze RASHE TN25 47 F2
Manor Ms DEAL CT14 12 D2
Manor Ri DVW CT17 58 A1
Manor Rd DEAL CT14 9 E5
DVW CT17 58 A1
FOLK CT20 6 D4
Manor Rw TENT TN30 * 70 B5
Manor Wy ASH TN23 2 C1
Manse Fld RASHE TN25 46 D2
Mansion Gdns DVE/WH CT16 22 A5
Mantles Hl DEAL CT14 10 B3
Maple Cl ASH TN23 28 B2
Maple Dr RFOLK CT18 35 F4
Maplefield Gdns RFOLK CT18 35 F4
Mardol Rd KEN/WIL TN24 19 E4
Maresfield Cl DVE/WH CT16 38 B2
Margaret St FOLK CT20 7 G4
Marina Ct DEAL CT14 * 9 H1
The Marina DEAL CT14 9 H1
Marine Crs FOLK CT20 7 G6
Marine Pde DVE/WH CT16 5 F6
FOLK CT20 7 G5
Marine Parade Ms FOLK CT20 7 G5
Marine Rd DEAL CT14 9 H5
Marine Ter FOLK CT20 7 G5
Marine Walk St HYTHE CT21 * 65 E5
Marjan Cl DVW CT17 38 A3
Market Hl HYTHE CT21 * 65 E5
Market St DEAL CT14 9 H3
Markland Rd DVW CT17 37 H5
Marlborough Rd DEAL CT14 11 E2
DVW CT17 37 H5
Marlborough Wy KEN/WIL TN24 19 H2
Marler Rd FOLKN CT19 67 E1
Marlowe Rd ASH TN23 2 E3
DVE/WH CT16 38 B1
Marmion Wy ASH TN23 28 A4
Marshalls Land TENT TN30 70 B1
Marsh La DEAL CT14 9 E3
Marsh Rd RASHW TN26 72 B5
Marsh Vw HYTHE CT21 74 A2
Martello Cots HYTHE CT21 * 74 D1
Martello Dr HYTHE CT21 74 C1
Martello Rd FOLK CT20 7 H2
FOLK CT20 66 D4
Martello Ter FOLK CT20 67 F4
Marten Rd FOLK CT20 6 A4
Martha Cl FOLKN CT19 53 H5
Martin Dale Crs RDV CT15 12 A5
Martins Cl TENT TN30 70 D4
Martin's Wy HYTHE CT21 74 B2
Mary Rd DEAL CT14 11 E1
Masons Rd DVW CT17 38 A3
Matthews Cl DEAL CT14 9 G3
Matthew's Pl DVE/WH CT16 4 C2
Maunsell Pl KEN/WIL TN24 29 H5
Maxton Rd DVW CT17 58 A1
Maxwell Pl DEAL CT14 9 G5
Mayers Rd DEAL CT14 11 E3
Mayfield Av DVE/WH CT16 38 B2
Mayfield Gdns DVE/WH CT16 38 B2
Mayfield Rd DVE/WH CT16 22 A2
RFOLK CT18 33 E3
Mayfly Dr RFOLK CT18 34 D5
Mayhew Cl ASH TN23 29 E4
Maypits ASH TN23 28 D4
Maypole Cl RFOLK CT18 35 E3
Maypole Gv RFOLK CT18 * 35 E4
The Meade RFOLK CT18 34 C5
Meadowbrook FOLK CT20 67 E3
Meadowbrook Cl KEN/WIL TN24 19 F3
Meadowbrook Ct FOLK CT20 * 67 E3
Meadowbrook Rd
KEN/WIL TN24 19 F3
Meadow Cl RFOLK CT18 35 E5
Meadow Ct HYTHE CT21 63 F1
Meadow Gv RASHE TN25 48 B4
Meadow Rd ASH TN23 18 C5
Meadow Vw RASHW TN26 16 D3
Meadow Wy HYTHE CT21 74 B2
Mead Rd FOLKN CT19 7 F1
KEN/WIL TN24 30 A5
Meadway DVW CT17 37 F1
Megone Cl RFOLK CT18 34 D5
Melbourne Av DVE/WH CT16 22 B4
Melcombe Cl ASH TN23 28 A5
Mendip KEN/WIL TN24 18 D5
Menzies Av DEAL CT14 11 F3
Menzies Rd DVE/WH CT16 21 H5
Merino Wy ASH TN23 42 C2
Meryl Gdns DEAL CT14 11 G3
Metropole Rd East FOLK CT20 6 A6
Metropole Rd West FOLK CT20 6 A7
Middelburg Sq FOLK CT20 6 E4
Middle Cl ASH TN23 28 A3
Middle Deal Rd DEAL CT14 9 E4
Middle Md FOLKN CT19 53 H5
Middle Rw KEN/WIL TN24 3 G3
Middle St ASH TN23 3 F4
DEAL CT14 9 H2
Midsummer Hl KEN/WIL TN24 19 F3
Milestone Cl FOLKN CT19 53 G5
Milestone Rd DEAL CT14 9 F4
Military Rd DVW CT17
DVW CT17
FOLK CT20
HYTHE CT21
Millais Rd DVE/WH CT16
Millbank Rd ASH TN23
Mill Bay FOLK CT20
Millbrook HYTHE CT21 *
Millbrook Meadow ASH TN23
Mill Cl DVW CT17
Mill Ct KEN/WIL TN24
Milldale Cl DEAL CT14
Miller Cl KEN/WIL TN24
Millfield ASH TN23
FOLK CT20
RDV CT15
RFOLK CT18
Millfield Cl RFOLK CT18
Mill Fields Rd HYTHE CT21
Mill Hl ASH TN23 *
DEAL CT14
Mill La DVE/WH CT16
DVE/WH CT16
KEN/WIL TN24
RFOLK CT18
TENT TN30
Mill Ms DEAL CT14
Mill Race DVW CT17
Mill Rd DEAL CT14
HYTHE CT21
RASHW TN26
Millstream Gn KEN/WIL TN24
Mill St DVE/WH CT16
Mill Vw KEN/WIL TN24
Milne Rd KEN/WIL TN24
Milton Cl DVE/WH CT16
Milton Rd ASH TN23
DVE/WH CT16
Minerva Av DVE/WH CT16
Minnis La DVW CT17
RDV CT15
Minnis Ter DVW CT17 *
Minter Av RFOLK CT18
Minter Cl RFOLK CT18
Mitchell Av RFOLK CT18
Mitchell St FOLKN CT19 *
Moat Farm Cl FOLKN CT19
Moat Farm Rd FOLKN CT19
Moatfield Meadow ASH TN23
Molloy Rd RASHW TN26
Monastery Av DVE/WH CT16
Mongeham Church Cl DEAL CT14
Mongeham Rd DEAL CT14
Monins Rd DVW CT17
Monks Wy DVE/WH CT16
Montcalm Ter DVE/WH CT16 *
Montfort Cl ASH TN23
Montgomery Wy FOLKN CT19
Montreal Cl DVE/WH CT16
Monument Wy KEN/WIL TN24
Moorstock La RASHE TN25
Morehall Av FOLKN CT19
Moreton Ter RASHW TN26 *
Morrison Rd FOLK CT20
Mortimer Cl ASH TN23
Mortimer Rd DVE/WH CT16
Mountbatten Wy RASHE TN25
Mount Pleasant DVW CT17 *
TENT TN30
Mountpleasant Cl RFOLK CT18
Mount Pleasant Rd FOLK CT20
Mount Rd DVW CT17
Mounts Cl DEAL CT14
Mount St HYTHE CT21
Mounts Vw RASHE TN25
Moyle Ct HYTHE CT21 *
Mulberry Ct HYTHE CT21 *
Mulberry Rd ASH TN23
Muscovy Rd RASHE TN25
Musgrove ASH TN23
Myrtle Gn ASH TN23
Myrtle Gv ASH TN23 *
Myrtle Rd FOLKN CT19

N

Naildown Cl HYTHE CT21
Naildown Rd HYTHE CT21
Nairne Cl RASHW TN26
Namur Pl RDV CT15
Napchester Rd DVE/WH CT16
Napier Gdns HYTHE CT21
Napier Rd DVE/WH CT16
Narrabeen Rd FOLKN CT19
Naseby Av FOLK CT20
Nash Hl RFOLK CT18
Natal Rd DVE/WH CT16
Neason Wy FOLKN CT19
Nelson Cl KEN/WIL TN24
Nelson Park Rd RDV CT15
Nelson St DEAL CT14
Nelson Ter DVE/WH CT16 *
Nettlefield KEN/WIL TN24
Nevill Gdns DEAL CT14
Newbury Cl FOLK CT20
New Dover Rd RFOLK CT18
Newenden Cl ASH TN23
Newington Rd RFOLK CT18
Newlands ASH TN23
DVE/WH CT16
Newlands Dr DEAL CT14
Newmans Cl HYTHE CT21
New Rectory La ASH TN23
New Rents ASH TN23
New Rd HYTHE CT21
RCANTW CT4
New St DEAL CT14
DVW CT17
FOLK CT20
KEN/WIL TN24
New Town Gn KEN/WIL TN24
Newtown Rd ASH TN23
New Town Rd KEN/WIL TN24
Nicholas Rd RASHE TN25
Nickley Wood Rd RASHW TN26 6
Nightingale Av HYTHE CT21
Nightingale Cl KEN/WIL TN24

ightingale Rd DVE/WH CT16.....38 C2
e Acres ASH/WH TN24.....28 A3
n La ASH TN23.....28 A3
ah's Ark Rd DVW CT17.....38 A4
ahs Ark Ter DVW CT17.....4 B7
akes Meadow ASH TN23.....2 B7
rfolk Dr ASH TN23.....29 C5
rman Rd ASH TN23.....29 C5
RDV CT15.....25 F4
rman St DVW CT17.....4 D4
rrington Md FOLK CT19.....53 G5
rthampton Quay DVW CT17.....4 D4
rth Barrack Rd DEAL CT14.....9 H5
rth Barracks DEAL CT14.....9 H5
rthbourne Av DVW CT17.....38 B4
rthbrooke Rd ASH/WH TN24.....3 G1
rthbrooke La KEN/WIL TN24.....3 G1
rth Camber Wy DVE/WH CT16.....39 H3
rth Cliff DEAL CT14.....66 D3
rthcote Rd DEAL CT14.....9 H4
DEAL CT14.....13 H3
rthdown KEN/WIL TN24.....19 E5
rth Downs Wy DVW CT17.....4 C6
HYTHE CT21.....7 F3
RASHE TN25.....14 C1
rth Downs Way
& Saxon Shore Wy RFOLK CT18.....3 G2
rth Exit Rd DVE/WH CT16.....39 G4
rthlands HYTHE CT21 *.....65 G5
rth La FOLK CT20.....67 E4
rth Lea DEAL CT14.....9 H2
rth Lyminge La RFOLK CT18.....33 E2
rth Military Rd DVW CT17.....4 C6
rth Pends KEN/WIL TN24.....3 G1
rth Return Rd DVE/WH CT16.....39 H4
rth Rd DEAL CT14.....13 H3
DVW CT17.....4 A6
rth St DEAL CT14.....9 H2
FOLKN CT19.....7 H4
OLKN TN24.....3 G2
thumberland Av
EN/WIL TN24.....19 F4
chwall Ms DEAL CT14.....9 G2
chwall Quay DVW CT17.....58 D1
thwall DEAL CT14.....9 G2
ton La RASHW TN26.....45 C3
way Dro RDV CT15.....25 E1
wood Gdns ASH TN23.....2 F4
wood St ASH TN23.....54 C2
sery Cl RFOLK CT18.....53 F1
sery La DVE/WH CT16.....21 H2
ey Cl KEN/WIL TN24.....3 H1

O

Dr RFOLK CT18.....35 E4
enpole ASH TN23.....28 C3
field Rd KEN/WIL TN24.....19 F5
ands ASH TN23.....2 A6
ASHE TN25.....45 G3
Rdg RASHW TN26.....73 G5
k FOLK CT20.....66 D1
ENT TN30.....70 D5
St DEAL CT14.....9 H3
Vw HYTHE CT21.....74 A2
Tree Rd ASH TN23.....2 B7
vale Cl DVW CT17.....38 B5
M HYTHE CT21.....65 E5
Meadow KEN/WIL TN24.....30 B3
vian Dr HYTHE CT21.....63 E4
Rd DVW CT17.....4 A6
ampton Cl KEN/WIL TN24.....19 H2
ash Cl RFOLK CT18.....35 G3
charlton Rd DVE/WH CT16.....55 D3
over Rd RFOLK CT18.....55 C5
olkestone Rd DVW CT17.....58 A3
ld High St FOLK CT20.....66 A5
ondon Rd HYTHE CT21.....64 A5
rd FOLK CT19.....53 G5
rch ASH TN23.....28 B4
ark Av DVE/WH CT16.....38 A1
ark Cl DVE/WH CT16.....22 A5
ark Hl DVE/WH CT16.....22 A5
ark Rd DVW CT17.....38 B2
ond Rd ASH TN23.....2 B6
ectory Cl RASHE TN25.....45 G2
OLK CT18.....9 H3
d RCANTW CT4.....27 H2
oman Rd RDV CT15.....24 A1
chool Ms FOLK CT20 *.....67 E4
airs Rd DEAL CT14.....13 G4
urrenden Manor Rd
RSHW TN26.....41 C1
nnery Ct TENT TN30 *.....70 A5
carage Gdns RASHE TN25.....15 E2
ard Av DEAL CT14.....9 G2
rd Cl DVE/WH CT16.....21 H1
d RASHE TN25.....45 G4
rd Fld HYTHE CT21 *.....65 E3
SHE TN25.....15 E3
rd Fld FOLK CT20.....40 A2
SHE TN25.....40 A2
rd Hts RASHE TN25.....9 B4
rd La RASHE TN25.....19 H3
rd Ms DEAL CT14 *.....9 B4
rd Rd TENT TN30.....70 B1
rchards RCANTW CT4.....27 H2
rd Va HYTHE CT21.....64 D5
rd Va TENT TN30.....70 D5
rchids RASHE TN25.....45 F3
LK CT18.....33 F5
Wy KEN/WIL TN24.....30 A4
e Rd FOLK CT20.....66 D1
HE CT21.....7 H2
Cl RASHE TN25.....46 D1
RFOLK CT18.....34 C4
ne Rd DEAL CT14.....13 G1
J/WIL TN24.....3 G4
Fld RASHE TN25.....19 G2
sier Rd RASHE TN25 *.....19 G2
Cl RFOLK CT18.....53 F1
d Pl DVW CT17.....38 B2
d Rd DVW CT17.....38 B2

Ottawa Crs DVE/WH CT16.....38 C2
Otterden Cl ASH TN23.....42 D1
Otterpool La RASHE TN25.....62 C2
Owen's Cl HYTHE CT21.....66 A4
Owen Sq DEAL CT14.....11 F2
Oxenden Rd FOLK CT20.....66 E3
Oxen Lease ASH TN23.....28 C4
Oxenturn Rd RASHE TN25.....15 E5
Oxford Ter FOLK CT20.....7 F5
Ox La TENT TN30.....70 D2

P

Paddock Cl DEAL CT14.....8 D4
FOLK CT20.....67 F2
The Paddocks ASH TN23.....28 A3
RFOLK CT18.....34 D1
The Paddock DVE/WH CT16.....4 E3
Padwell La ASH TN23.....28 A4
Page Pl FOLKN CT19.....54 B4
Page Rd RFOLK CT18.....53 F1
Palmbeach HYTHE CT21.....74 B2
Palmerston Av DEAL CT14.....11 G1
Palmerston Rd DVE/WH CT16.....4 E5
Palmerston St DVW CT17.....6 E2
Palm Tree Wy RFOLK CT18.....32 D2
Palting Wy FOLK CT20.....6 D5
Pannell Dr RFOLK CT18.....34 C5
Papper La KEN/WIL TN24.....44 B1
Papworth Cl FOLKN CT19.....53 C5
Parade Rd FOLK CT20.....67 E4
The Parade DEAL CT14.....44 B2
Paraker Wy HYTHE CT21.....66 B4
Pardoners Wy DVE/WH CT16.....38 A1
Parfitt Wy DVE/WH CT16.....38 B2
Park Av DEAL CT14.....9 F4
DVE/WH CT16.....4 A6
Park Cl RFOLK CT18.....34 D5
Park Dr RASHW TN26.....17 E3
Parker Pl RFOLK CT18.....35 F4
Park Farm Rd FOLKN CT19.....53 C4
Parkfield Rd RFOLK CT18.....34 D5
Park La RCANTW CT4.....27 F1
Park Lea DEAL CT14 *.....9 G4
Park Ms DVE/WH CT16.....4 D5
Park Pl ASH TN23.....29 C5
DVE/WH CT16.....4 D5
KEN/WIL TN24.....30 B3
Park Rd DVE/WH CT16.....21 F4
FOLK CT19.....67 E1
HYTHE CT21.....75 E1
KEN/WIL TN24.....30 C3
Park Rd North KEN/WIL TN24.....3 G2
Parkside DEAL CT14 *.....9 G3
Park St DEAL CT14.....9 F3
DVE/WH CT16.....4 D5
KEN/WIL TN24.....30 C3
Park V KEN/WIL TN24.....19 F3
Park Vw FOLKN CT19.....54 C5
Park Wood Cl ASH TN23.....43 F4
The Parsonage RDV CT15 *.....24 D4
The Pasture ASH TN23.....19 F5
RFOLK CT18.....35 E5
Patterson Cl DEAL CT14.....9 H3
Paul's Pl DVE/WH CT16.....4 C2
The Pavement TENT TN30.....70 B1
Pavilion Cl DEAL CT14 *.....9 F4
Pavilion Meadow DVW CT17.....21 F5
Pavilion Rd FOLKN CT19.....6 E2
Paxton Av RFOLK CT18.....53 F1
Payers Pk FOLK CT20.....7 G4
Pay St RFOLK CT18.....34 B2
Pegden RCANTW CT4 *.....27 H1
Pelham Gdns FOLK CT20.....67 G3
Pemberton Rd KEN/WIL TN24.....3 J4
Pembury Pl RASHE TN25.....18 B5
Pencester Ct DVE/WH CT16 *.....4 E4
Pencester Rd DVE/WH CT16.....4 E4
Penderel Ms TENT TN30.....70 C4
Penfold Rd FOLKN CT19.....7 J2
Penn Hl ASH TN23.....42 C1
Pennine Wy KEN/WIL TN24.....19 H1
Pent Vale Cl FOLKN CT19.....67 G1
Percival Ter DVW CT17.....4 A5
Peregrine Cl HYTHE CT21.....74 B2
Perries Md FOLKN CT19.....53 C5
Perrot Wy RFOLK CT18.....35 F4
Peter Candier Wy
KEN/WIL TN24.....19 G5
Peter St DEAL CT14.....9 G3
DVE/WH CT16.....4 C2
FOLK CT20.....66 D3
Peverell Rd DVE/WH CT16.....4 C2
Pharos Dr DVE/WH CT16.....5 F2
Phillip Rd FOLKN CT19.....67 E1
The Pier DVE/WH CT16.....21 H1
Pike Cl FOLK CT19.....5 C5
Pilgrim Spring FOLK CT20.....54 A4
Pilgrims Wy DVE/WH CT16.....38 A1
Pilots Av DEAL CT14.....9 E5
Pineham Rd RDV CT15.....22 D3
Pine Wy FOLK CT20.....52 D5
Pioneer Rd DVE/WH CT16.....38 A1
Pittlesden TENT TN30.....70 B5
Pittlesden Pl TENT TN30.....70 B5
Pixwell La DEAL CT14.....10 B1
Plain Cots FOLK CT20 *.....67 G3
Plain Rd FOLK CT20.....47 E2
RASHE TN25.....47 E2
Plantation RASHW TN26.....17 E2
Pleydell Gdns FOLK CT20.....6 D6
Plimsol Av FOLK CT20.....52 D5
Plough Hl RDV CT15.....56 B3
Ploughmans Wy ASH TN23.....42 B2
Plover Rd RFOLK CT18.....53 F1
Pluckley Rd RASHW TN26.....16 A5
Poets Wk DEAL CT14.....11 F5
Pollard Cl ASH TN23.....42 A3
Pommeus La DEAL CT14.....10 B5
Poncia Rd ASH TN23.....29 C5
Pond Hill Rd FOLK CT20.....66 C5
Pond La RDV CT15.....24 B3

Pondmore Wy RASHE TN25.....18 B5
Poplar Cl ASH TN23.....29 A2
The Poplars ASH TN23 *.....29 A2
Portland Cl FOLK CT20.....64 D5
KEN/WIL TN24.....18 D2
Portland Rd HYTHE CT21.....64 D5
Postling ASH TN23.....43 F5
Postling Rd FOLK CT19.....53 E5
Potters Cl RASHE TN25.....18 A4
Poulton Cl DVW CT17.....37 H4
Pound Cl DEAL CT14.....8 D4
Pound La ASH TN23.....47 F2
RASHE TN25.....47 F2
RCANTW CT4.....27 H2
Pound Wy FOLK CT20.....7 F5
Prescott Cl DVW CT17.....23 E4
Primrose Dr ASH TN23.....43 F5
Primrose Rd DVW CT17.....38 A3
Prince of Wales Rbt DVW CT17.....4 D7
Princes Pde HYTHE CT21.....65 H5
Princes St FOLK CT19.....7 H4
Princes St DEAL CT14.....9 F3
DVW CT17.....4 E5
Princes Ter HYTHE CT21 *.....74 D1
Prince William Ct DEAL CT14 *.....9 F2
Priory Gdns FOLK CT20.....7 G5
Priory Gate Rd DVW CT17.....4 C4
Priory Gv DVW CT17.....4 C4
Priory Hl DVW CT17.....4 B4
Priory Rd DVW CT17.....4 B4
Priory Station Approach Rd
DVW CT17.....4 C4
Priory St DVW CT17.....4 C4
Priory Wy TENT TN30.....70 D5
Pritchard Dr RFOLK CT18.....34 D5
Proctor Wk RFOLK CT18.....34 D5
Prospect Ms HYTHE CT21 *.....65 E5
Prospect Pl DVW CT17.....38 B3
Prospect Rd FOLK CT20.....66 E4
HYTHE CT21.....65 E5
Prospect Wy RASHE TN25.....18 A5
Providence St ASH TN23.....29 C4
Puffin Ct RFOLK CT18.....53 G1

Q

Quantock Dr KEN/WIL TN24.....2 E1
Quarrington La RASHE TN25.....31 H4
Quarry Rd HYTHE CT21.....64 D4
Quarry Vw ASH TN23.....26 D5
Quarry Wk HYTHE CT21.....64 D4
Quebec Ter DVE/WH CT16 *.....38 B1
Queen Elizabeth Rd DVE/WH
CT16.....5 H4
Queens Av DVW CT17.....37 H5
FOLK CT20.....66 B1
Queens Ct KEN/WIL TN24.....3 G2
Queensdown Rd DEAL CT14.....13 G5
Queen's Gdns DVW CT17.....4 E4
Queens Ms DEAL CT14.....9 F4
FOLK CT20.....66 B1
Queen's Ri DEAL CT14.....12 D2
Queens Rd DEAL CT14.....9 F4
Queen's Rd KEN/WIL TN24.....30 C3
Queens Road Upper
KEN/WIL TN24.....3 F1
Queen St DEAL CT14.....9 G3
DVE/WH CT16.....4 E5
FOLK CT20.....7 G3
Queen Victoria Rw
DVE/WH CT16 *.....4 D4
Quern Rd DEAL CT14.....12 D1
Quested Rd FOLKN CT19.....67 E1
Quince Orch RASHW TN26.....72 B4

Rendezvous St FOLK CT20.....7 G4
Repton Manor Rd ASH TN23.....28 A5
Ribston Wy ASH TN23.....28 A5
Richborough Wy ASH TN23.....42 C2
Richmond St FOLKN CT19.....66 D1
The Ridge KEN/WIL TN24.....19 G3
Ridgeway HYTHE CT21.....63 E4
The Ridgeway DVW CT17.....37 G2
RASHE TN25.....46 B2
Riding Hl KEN/WIL TN24.....19 E3
Rigden Rd ASH TN23.....29 C4
Ringwould Rd RDV CT15.....12 B3
Ripley Rd KEN/WIL TN24.....30 C4
Ripple Rd DEAL CT14.....12 C1
Risborough La FOLK CT20.....66 D2
Risborough Wy FOLK CT20.....67 E1
The Rise ASH TN23.....28 C5
DEAL CT14.....13 G2
RDV CT15.....25 F4
Rising Rd ASH TN23.....2 C6
Riverbank Wy KEN/WIL TN24.....19 F5
River Di DVW CT17.....37 H1
River Dr DVW CT17.....37 H2
River Meadow DVW CT17.....37 H1
Riversdale Rd ASH TN23.....29 C4
Riverside DVE/WH CT16.....21 F4
Riverside DEAL CT14.....13 G1
River St DVW CT17.....37 C1
Riverview ASH TN23.....28 C3
Riviera Rd FOLK CT20.....67 F4
Road of Remembrance
FOLK CT20.....7 F5
Robert St DEAL CT14.....9 F4
Robin's Cl HYTHE CT21.....74 A2
Robus Cl RFOLK CT18.....33 E2
Rogersmead TENT TN30.....70 A5
Rokesley Rd DVE/WH CT16.....22 A5
Roman Cl DEAL CT14.....9 F3
Roman Rd DVE/WH CT16.....38 D2
FOLKN CT19.....66 C1
Roman Wy ASH TN23.....43 D5
FOLKN CT19.....66 C1
Romney Av FOLK CT20.....67 F2
Romney Marsh Rd ASH TN23.....3 G6
Romney Point ASH TN23.....18 B5
Romney Rd ASH TN23.....30 A3
RASHE TN25.....72 B4
Romney Wy HYTHE CT21.....74 C1
Romsey Cl FOLKN CT19.....30 C2
Romulus Gdns ASH TN23.....42 D3
Rookery Cl KEN/WIL TN24.....19 F2
Roosevelt Rd DVE/WH CT16.....38 B1
Roselands DEAL CT14.....11 F5
Rose Vls ASH TN23.....3 G7
Rose Wk RFOLK CT18.....34 D5
Rosewood Dr RASHE TN25.....18 A5
Rossendale Gdns FOLK CT20.....7 H2
Rossendale Rd FOLK CT20.....7 H2
Ross Wy FOLK CT20.....52 E5
Rothbrook Dr KEN/WIL TN24.....19 E2
Rothley Cl TENT TN30.....70 C4
Rowan Cl ASH TN23.....28 C2
The Row RCANTW CT4.....27 H2
Royal Blds DEAL CT14 *.....9 H5
Royal Military Av FOLK CT20.....66 D2
Royal Military Canal Pth
RASHE TN26.....73 H3
Royds Rd ASH TN23.....28 B5
Royston Gdns RDV CT15.....24 D4
Ruckinge Rd RASHW TN26.....72 B4
Ruffets Wd ASH TN23.....43 G4
Rugby Gdns ASH TN23.....29 G4
Rugby Rd DVW CT17.....58 A1
Running Foxes La ASH TN23.....26 D5
Rural Ter RASHE TN25 *.....15 E2
Russell Rd FOLKN CT19.....6 D1
Russell St ASH TN23.....5 F4
Russett Cl ASH TN23.....28 A5
Rutherford Rd RASHE TN25.....18 B5
Rutland Rd DVE/WH CT16.....38 B1
Ryland Pl DVW CT17.....7 H5
Rylands Rd KEN/WIL TN24.....19 F5

R

Radnor Bridge Rd FOLK CT20.....7 H3
Radnor Cliff FOLK CT20.....7 G5
Radnor Cliff Crs FOLK CT20.....67 F5
Radnor Park Av FOLKN CT19.....6 D2
Radnor Park Gdns FOLKN CT19.....6 D2
Radnor Park Rd FOLKN CT19.....6 D2
Radnor Pk West FOLKN CT19.....6 B3
Radnor St FOLKN CT19.....7 G4
Raleigh Cl KEN/WIL TN24.....30 C4
Ram La HDCN TN27.....16 A1
Ramstone Cl RASHE TN25.....47 E2
Randolph Gdns KEN/WIL TN24.....19 G4
Randolph Rd DVW CT17.....4 A3
Ranelagh Rd DEAL CT14.....9 F4
Range Rd HYTHE CT21.....75 E1
Ravenna Rd FOLK CT20.....67 G2
Ravenscourt Rd DEAL CT14.....9 G4
Raymond Fuller Wy
KEN/WIL TN24.....19 G5
Reach Cl RDV CT15.....24 D4
Reachfields HYTHE CT21.....75 E1
Reach Rd HYTHE CT21.....62 B5
RDV CT15.....24 D4
Readers Bridge Rd TENT TN30.....70 A1
Reading Cl DEAL CT14.....11 F3
Reading Rd DVW CT17.....37 H5
Recreation Ground Rd
TENT TN30.....70 C5
Rectory La HYTHE CT21.....64 D5
Rectory Rd DEAL CT14.....44 C4
Rectory Wy KEN/WIL TN24.....19 E4
Red Barn La ASH TN23.....36 A1
Redbrooks Wy HYTHE CT21.....74 A1
Redbrook St RFOLK CT18.....67 E2
Redsull Av DEAL CT14.....11 E1
Red Tree Orch ASH TN23.....28 C5
Redwing Rd RFOLK CT18.....53 G1
Redyear Ct ASH TN23.....30 C5
Reed Crs ASH TN23.....42 A3
Reedmace Cl ASH TN23.....28 B4
Regents Ct ASH TN23.....2 E3
Regents Pl ASH TN23.....2 E3
Remus Cl ASH TN23.....42 D3

S

Sabre Crs ASH TN23.....28 B5
Sackville Cl RASHW TN26.....17 E3
Sackville Crs ASH TN23.....2 C3
Saddlers Wy ASH TN23.....43 C4
Saffron's Pl DEAL CT14.....7 H4
St Alphege Rd DVE/WH CT16.....4 C1
St Ambrose Gn RASHE TN25.....15 E2
St Andrews Cl HYTHE CT21.....53 H5
St Andrews Gdns DVW CT17 *.....38 B2
St Andrews Rd DEAL CT14.....9 G3
St Anne's Rd ASH TN23.....28 B5
St Augustines Rd DVW CT17.....8 D5
St Bart's DVW CT17 *.....4 B3
St Benets Wy TENT TN30.....70 D4
St Clare Rd DEAL CT14.....11 G3
St Davids Av DVW CT17.....58 A3
St David's Rd DEAL CT14.....11 G3
St Denys Rd RFOLK CT18.....35 E4
St Eanswythe Wy FOLK CT20.....7 F4
St Edmund's Rd DEAL CT14.....11 G3
St Francis Cl DEAL CT14.....28 D5
St Francis Ct ASH TN23.....28 D5
St Francis Rd DEAL CT14.....11 G3
St Georges Crs DVW CT17 *.....38 A2
St Georges Crs DVW CT17.....58 B2
St George's Pl HYTHE CT21.....74 B2
St Georges Pl RDV CT15.....24 D4
St George's Rd DEAL CT14.....10 H3
FOLKN CT19.....67 F1
St Giles Rd DVW CT17.....58 B2
St Giles Wk DVW CT17.....58 B2
St Gregory's Cl DEAL CT14.....44 B4
St Hilda Rd FOLKN CT19.....67 E1
St Hilda's Rd HYTHE CT21.....75 F1
St Hugh Ter RFOLK CT18 *.....34 C5
St James La DVE/WH CT16.....5 F5
St James Rd DEAL CT14.....13 G2
St John's Church Rd FOLKN CT19.....6 D2
St John's Cl RFOLK CT18.....34 D2
St Johns Cl KEN/WIL TN24.....44 D1
St Johns La KEN/WIL TN24.....3 G4

St John's Rd DVW CT17 ....4 C5
St Johns Rd HYTHE CT21 ....64 C4
St John's St FOLK CT20 ....7 G3
St John's Wy RFOLK CT18 ....34 C2
St Lawrence Ter DVE/WH CT16 * 9 B1
St Leonards Rd DEAL CT14 ....9 F5
St Leonards Rd HYTHE CT21 ....35 F1
St Luke's Wk RFOLK CT18 ....34 C5
St Margarets Dr DEAL CT14 ....11 F3
St Margarets Rd RDV CT15 ....13 E5
St Margarets Rd RDV CT15 ....25 C5
St Mark's Cl DEAL CT14 ....66 D2
St Martin's Cl DVW CT17 ....58 B2
St Martins Gdns DVW CT17 * 4 C1
St Martins Rd DEAL CT14 ....8 D5
    FOLK CT20 ....66 D1
St Martin's Rd RDV CT17 ....23 E5
St Marys Cl RASHW TN26 ....72 B3
St Marys Cl RFOLK CT18 ....51 F1
St Marys Ct RFOLK CT18 ....10 C5
St Marys Gn KEN/WIL TN24 ....19 G2
St Marys Ms KEN/WIL TN24 ....30 B4
St Marys Rd DEAL CT14 ....11 G3
St Michael's Cl DEAL CT14 8
St Michael's Ter TENT TN30 * 70 B1
St Michaels Wk RFOLK CT18 ....34 C5
St Mildred's Cl DEAL CT14 ....9 G3
St Mildreds Ct DEAL CT14 ....11 G3
St Monicas Rd DEAL CT14 ....13 H1
St Nicholas Cl DEAL CT14 8
St Nicholas Rd HYTHE CT21 ....64 C5
St Patricks Cl DEAL CT14 ....9 G5
St Patricks Rd DVW CT17 ....58 A3
St Paul's Wy FOLK CT20 ....38 A5
St Radigund's Rd DVW CT17 ....38 A3
St Richards Rd DEAL CT14 ....11 E2
St Saviours Cl FOLKN CT19 ....54 B5
St Stephen's Ms ASH TN23 ....43 E1
St Stephen's Wk ASH TN23 ....28 D5
St Stephens Wy FOLK CT20 ....67 E3
St Theresas Cl HYTHE CT21 ....2 E2
St Vincent Rd RDV CT15 ....24 C3
St Winifred Rd FOLKN CT19 ....57 F1
Salisbury Rd DEAL CT14 ....11 F2
    DVE/WH CT16 ....4 D2
    FOLKN CT19 ....53 E5
    RDV CT15 ....7 F5
Samian Crs FOLKN CT19 ....66 C1
Samphire Ct DVE/WH CT16 ....5 F3
Sanctuary Cl DVW CT17 ....21 F5
Sandgate Hl FOLK CT20 ....67 F4
Sandgate Rd FOLK CT20 ....6 B6
Sandilands KEN/WIL TN24 ....30 A5
Sandling Rd HYTHE CT21 ....64 B1
The Sandlings HYTHE CT21 * 74 A2
Sandpiper Rd RFOLK CT18 ....53 G1
Sandwich Ct DVW CT17 ....4 A2
Sandwich Rd DVE/WH CT16 ....22 A2
Sandyhurst La RASHE TN25 ....18 A3
Sandy La FOLK CT20 ....66 C4
    HYTHE CT21 ....30 D5
    KEN/WIL TN24 ....3 G5
    TENT TN30 ....70 C5
Sandy Pl RASHE TN25 ....46 D2
Sassoon Cl RFOLK CT18 ....34 D5
Satmar La RFOLK CT18 ....55 H1
    RFOLK CT18 ....55 H1
Saw Lodge Fld ASH TN23 ....43 G3
Saxon Cl HYTHE CT21 ....65 G5
Saxon Shore Wy DEAL CT14 ....11 H4
    DVE/WH CT16 ....5 F6
    HYTHE CT21 ....62 C5
    RASHW TN26 ....72 C2
    RDV CT15 ....25 G4
    RFOLK CT18 ....33 E5
Saxon St DVW CT17 ....4 D4
Sayers La TENT TN30 ....70 B5
Scanlons Bridge Rd HYTHE CT21 ....64 A5
School La RFOLK CT18 ....64 A5
School Rd HYTHE CT21 ....64 A3
    RASHW TN26 ....17 E2
    RASHW TN26 ....40 C5
    RFOLK CT18 ....34 B2
Scotland Common DVE/WH CT16 ....21 E5
Scotton St RASHE TN25 ....15 F2
Seabrook Ct HYTHE CT21 ....66 B4
Seabrook Gdns HYTHE CT21 ....66 A5
Seabrook Gv HYTHE CT21 ....66 A5
Seabrook V HYTHE CT21 ....66 A5
Seadown Cl HYTHE CT21 ....66 A3
Seagrave Crs FOLKN CT19 ....7 J3
Sea Rd DEAL CT14 ....13 G1
    HYTHE CT21 ....66 A5
Sea St RDV CT15 ....25 E4
Seaton Av HYTHE CT21 ....66 D4
Sea View Cl RFOLK CT18 ....55 F3
Sea View Ter FOLK CT20 * 66 D4
Segrave Rd FOLKN CT19 ....7 J3
Selkirk Rd DVE/WH CT16 ....5 F3
Selway Ct DEAL CT14 ....11 F1
Sene Pk HYTHE CT21 ....65 F5
Setterfield House HYTHE CT21 * 65 F5
Sevington La KEN/WIL TN24 ....30 A4
Seymour Rd DEAL CT14 ....24 D2
Shaftesbury Av FOLKN CT19 ....52 D5
Shakespeare Av DVW CT17 ....5 B1
Shakespeare Ter FOLK CT20 ....6 B5
Shaw Cross KEN/WIL TN24 ....19 F4
Shearway Rd FOLKN CT19 ....53 F5
Sheepfold La ASH TN23 ....9 G5
Sheffield Gdns DEAL CT14 ....11 G3
Sheldwich Cl ASH TN23 ....42 D1
Shellons St FOLK CT20 ....7 F4
Shepherd Cl ASH TN23 ....42 C2
Shepherd Dr KEN/WIL TN24 ....19 G4
Shepherds Wk HYTHE CT21 ....74 C2
Shepway KEN/WIL TN24 ....19 G4
Shepway Cl FOLKN CT19 ....7 F2
Sheridan Rd DVE/WH CT16 ....38 B1
Sheron Cl DEAL CT14 ....11 H4
Sherwood Cl KEN/WIL TN24 ....19 F2
Shipley Mill Cl ASH TN23 ....43 G3
Shipmans Wy DVE/WH CT16 ....38 A1
Ship St FOLKN CT19 ....6 E3
Shireway Cl FOLKN CT19 ....53 G5
Sholden Bank DEAL CT14 ....8 D3
Sholden New Rd DEAL CT14 ....8 D4
Shooter's Hl DVW CT17 ....4 B2
Shoreham La TENT TN30 ....70 B1
Shorncliffe Crs FOLK CT20 ....67 E2

Shorncliffe Rd FOLK CT20 ....6 C4
The Shrubbery DEAL CT14 ....11 G3
Shrubcote TENT TN30 ....70 D5
Shuttlesfield La RCANTW CT4 ....27 F5
The Sidings RFOLK CT18 ....33 E2
Sidney St FOLKN CT19 ....7 G1
Silecroft Ct ASH TN23 * 28 C5
Silver Birch Ct RASHW TN26 ....60 C1
Silver Birch Gv ASH TN23 ....43 F3
Silver Hill Gdns KEN/WIL TN24 ....30 C3
Silver Hill Rd KEN/WIL TN24 ....30 C3
Silverlands Rd RFOLK CT18 ....32 D2
Silver St DEAL CT14 ....9 H2
Simcoe Ter KEN/WIL TN24 ....38 B1
Simone Weil Av KEN/WIL TN24 ....18 D5
Simon's Av ASH TN23 ....28 C5
Singledge Av DVE/WH CT16 ....21 H5
Singledge La RDV CT15 ....21 G2
Singleton Hl ASH TN23 ....28 B4
Singleton Rd ASH TN23 ....28 A3
Sir John Fogge Av ASH TN23 ....18 D5
Sir John Moore Av HYTHE CT21 ....64 C5
Siskin Cl RASHE TN25 ....18 D2
    RFOLK CT18 ....34 B5
Six Fields Pth TENT TN30 ....70 B1
Skeete Rd RFOLK CT18 ....32 B2
Skylark Wy ASH TN23 ....43 E2
Smallhythe Rd TENT TN30 ....70 A5
Smithy Dr ASH TN23 ....43 G3
Snargate St DVW CT17 ....4 D7
Snipe Cl RASHE TN25 ....19 G2
Snowbell Rd ASH TN23 ....43 G3
Snowdrop Cl FOLKN CT19 ....54 A4
Somerset Rd DEAL CT14 ....11 F1
    FOLKN CT19 ....67 E1
    KEN/WIL TN24 ....30 C3
Sondes Rd DEAL CT14 ....9 H4
Sotherton KEN/WIL TN24 ....30 A5
Souberg Cl DEAL CT14 ....9 G1
Southbourne ASH TN23 ....42 C2
Southbourne Rd FOLKN CT19 ....7 J3
South Camber Wy DVE/WH CT16 ....39 H4
Southenay La RASHE TN25 ....44 A1
Southern Wy FOLK CT20 ....7 H2
Southernwood Ri FOLK CT20 ....67 F3
Southgate Rd TENT TN30 ....70 D5
South Lea ASH TN23 ....43 E4
Southmead Cl FOLKN CT19 ....7 F2
South Military Rd DVW CT17 ....58 C2
South Motto ASH TN23 ....43 F2
South Rd DEAL CT14 ....13 H2
    DVW CT17 ....4 A3
    HYTHE CT21 ....75 G1
South Stour Av ASH TN23 ....3 G7
South St DEAL CT14 ....9 E1
South Wall DEAL CT14 ....9 E1
Southwall Rd DEAL CT14 ....9 E1
Spanton Crs HYTHE CT21 ....65 F4
Speldhurst Cl ASH TN23 ....42 C2
Spence Cl RFOLK CT18 ....34 D5
Spencer Ct FOLK CT20 * 66 C5
Spindlewood End ASH TN23 ....17 H5
The Spinney ASH TN23 ....28 D5
    DVW CT17 ....37 G2
Spitfire Wy RFOLK CT18 ....53 H1
Springfield Av TENT TN30 ....70 D2
Springfield Rd DVE/WH CT16 * 38 B2
Springfield Rd RFOLK CT18 ....66 B3
Spring La HYTHE CT21 ....30 C3
Springside Ter RFOLK CT18 ....53 E3
Spring Ter FOLK CT20 * 7 F3
Springwood Cl ASH TN23 ....28 C1
Springwood Dr ASH TN23 ....28 B1
Sprotlands Av KEN/WIL TN24 ....30 B4
The Square RCANTW CT4 ....27 H2
Squires Wy DVE/WH CT16 ....38 A1
Squirrel La RASHE TN25 ....18 A5
Stablemead ASH TN23 ....53 G5
Stace Cl TENT TN30 ....70 C5
Stade St HYTHE CT21 ....65 E5
The Stade FOLKN CT19 ....7 J3
Stafford Cl DEAL CT14 ....2 B1
Stanbury Crs FOLKN CT19 ....54 D4
Standen La RFOLK CT18 ....35 G4
Stanhope Rd ASH TN23 ....9 H4
    DEAL CT14 ....9 H4
    DVE/WH CT16 ....38 C2
Stanley Rd DEAL CT14 ....9 G1
    FOLKN CT19 ....67 E1
Star La FOLKN CT19 ....52 D5
Star Rd KEN/WIL TN24 ....3 K4
Station Ap RDV CT15 ....12 A5
Station Dr DEAL CT14 ....11 E3
Station Rd ASH TN23 ....11 E1
    DEAL CT14 ....9 H2
    FOLKN CT19 ....67 E1
    HYTHE CT21 ....65 F5
    RASHE TN25 ....46 B4
    RDV CT15 ....25 E4
    RFOLK CT18 ....33 E3
    TENT TN30 ....70 B5
St Bartholemews Cl DVW CT17 ....4 B4
Steddy Cl ASH TN23 ....42 D1
Steeds Cl RASHW TN26 ....45 E5
Stembrook DVW CT17 * 4 D5
Stempe Cl RFOLK CT18 ....53 H1
Stiles Cl FOLKN CT19 ....53 G5
Stiring Rd ASH TN23 ....29 H5
Stockdale Gdns DEAL CT14 ....9 G3
Stock La RASHE TN25 ....46 A4
Stoddart Rd FOLKN CT19 ....67 E1
Stombers La RFOLK CT18 ....35 F3
Stonegate RASHE TN25 ....15 E2
Stonehall Rd RDV CT15 ....25 E4
Stone Hl ASH TN23 ....20 D5
Stone St HYTHE CT21 ....63 E5
    RASHE TN25 ....49 F4
Stour KEN/WIL TN24 ....43 H1
Stour Ct ASH TN23 ....28 C5
Stourfields ASH TN23 ....3 J5
Stour Valley Wk KEN/WIL TN24 ....2 A5
    RASHE TN25 ....14 D5
Stowell Cl ASH TN23 ....28 A4
The Strand DEAL CT14 ....11 H1
The Street ASH TN23 ....3 H8
    DEAL CT14 ....8 D4
    HYTHE CT21 ....50 B2
    HYTHE CT21 ....62 D5
    KEN/WIL TN24 ....19 G2

RASHW TN26 ....16 D3
RASHW TN26 ....40 C2
RASHW TN26 ....60 C2
RDV CT15 ....55 F1
RFOLK CT18 ....56 B2
RFOLK CT18 ....35 F4
RFOLK CT18 ....52 A5
Strond St DVW CT17 ....4 D7
Strouts Rd ASH TN23 ....28 B5
Stuart Ct DVW CT17 * 4 C4
Stuart Rd FOLKN CT19 ....7 J1
Studfall Cl HYTHE CT21 ....74 B2
Studio Cl KEN/WIL TN24 ....19 F3
Sturdy Cl HYTHE CT21 ....65 F5
Sturges Rd KEN/WIL TN24 ....3 F2
Suffolk Dr ASH TN23 ....2 C4
Sugar Loaf Wk RDV CT15 ....54 B4
Summer Cl HYTHE CT21 ....64 D5
    TENT TN30 ....70 D3
Summerhill Pk KEN/WIL TN24 ....31 E5
Summer Leeze KEN/WIL TN24 ....19 E5
Summer Leeze Gdns
    KEN/WIL TN24 ....30 A4
Sun La HYTHE CT21 ....64 A4
Sunningdale Av FOLKN CT19 ....53 G5
Sunny Bank HYTHE CT21 ....64 A5
Sunnyside Cl DEAL CT14 ....10 B3
Sunnyside Cots DEAL CT14 * 9 G3
Surrenden Rd FOLKN CT19 ....53 F5
Sussex Ct FOLKN CT19 ....44 A1
Sussex Av RFOLK CT18 ....2 F2
Sussex Rd FOLKN CT19 ....7 F2
Sutherland Cl HYTHE CT21 ....64 C5
Sutherland Rd DEAL CT14 ....9 G3
Sutton Cl HYTHE CT21 ....64 D5
Sutton La DEAL CT14 ....10 A2
Swaffer Wy ASH TN23 ....28 A5
Swain Rd TENT TN30 ....70 C1
Swallowfield KEN/WIL TN24 ....30 A5
Swan Gn RASHE TN25 ....46 A4
Swan La RASHE TN25 ....48 B5
Sweet Bay Crs ASH TN23 ....43 E4
Swiss Wy FOLKN CT19 ....54 D5
Sycamore Cl HYTHE CT21 ....74 C1
Sycamore La ASH TN23 ....18 A5
Sydcot Dr DEAL CT14 ....9 G1
Sydenham Rd DEAL CT14 ....9 H2
Sydney Rd DEAL CT14 ....11 E3
Sydney St ASH TN23 ....29 G4

T

Tabret Cl KEN/WIL TN24 ....19 F3
Tadworth Rd KEN/WIL TN24 ....19 F3
Tally Ho Rd RASHW TN26 ....60 D1
Tangier Cl RDV CT15 ....39 E1
Tanner's Hl HYTHE CT21 ....65 E3
Tanner's Hill Gdns HYTHE CT21 ....65 E3
Tannery La ASH TN23 ....3 H4
Target Firs DVE/WH CT16 ....31 F4
Taswell Cl DVE/WH CT16 ....5 F3
Taswell St DVE/WH CT16 ....5 F3
Taylor Rd FOLKN CT19 ....67 E1
Taylors Pas KEN/WIL TN24 ....28 A4
Taylors Yd RASHE TN25 ....15 E2
Taywood Cl KEN/WIL TN24 ....30 B3
Teal Cl RFOLK CT18 ....53 F1
Teddars Leas Rd RFOLK CT18 ....51 E3
Telegraph Rd DEAL CT14 ....11 F2
Telford Ct FOLKN CT19 ....7 G1
Temeraire Rd FOLK CT20 * 53 H1
Templar Dr DVE/WH CT16 ....21 F4
Templar St DVW CT17 ....4 B7
Temple Cl ASH TN23 ....42 D2
    DVE/WH CT16 ....21 F4
Templer Ms KEN/WIL TN24 ....2 B1
Temple Side DVE/WH CT16 ....21 F4
Tennyson Pl FOLKN CT19 ....54 D5
Tennyson Rd ASH TN23 ....43 E1
Terlingham La RFOLK CT18 ....53 G2
Thanet Gdns FOLKN CT19 ....7 J1
Thanet Ter RASHW TN26 * 17 E3
Theatre St HYTHE CT21 ....64 D5
Theresa Rd HYTHE CT21 ....75 F1
Thirlmere KEN/WIL TN24 ....19 E3
Thistledown DEAL CT14 ....11 H4
Thomas Cl ASH TN23 ....43 E1
Thompson Cl DEAL CT14 ....9 G1
    FOLKN CT19 ....53 H5
Thomson Rd KEN/WIL TN24 ....19 F3
Thornbridge Rd DEAL CT14 ....31 E1
Thornlea ASH TN23 ....28 C2
Thornton Cl KEN/WIL TN24 ....19 E1
Tilden Gill Rd TENT TN30 ....70 D5
Tile Kiln La FOLKN CT19 ....53 F5
Tile Kiln Rd KEN/WIL TN24 ....19 E2
Timperley Cl DEAL CT14 ....11 F3
Tithe Barn La ASH TN23 ....28 B4
Toll Ga DEAL CT14 ....8 E5
Tolsford Cl FOLKN CT19 ....3 K6
    RFOLK CT18 ....51 E1
Tontine St FOLK CT20 ....7 G3
Tormore Ms DEAL CT14 ....9 E5
Tormore Pk DEAL CT14 ....9 E5
Toronto Cl DVW CT17 ....38 B1
Torrington Pl ASH TN23 ....29 G4
Torrington Rd ASH TN23 ....28 D5
Tournay Cl ASH TN23 ....28 D4
Tourney Cl HYTHE CT21 ....62 D4
Tower Gdns HYTHE CT21 ....64 D5
Tower Hamlets Rd DVW CT17 ....4 B3
Tower Hamlets St DVW CT17 * 4 B4
Tower Hl DVW CT17 ....4 B4
Tower St DVW CT17 ....4 B4
Towers Vw KEN/WIL TN24 ....19 E2
Townsend Farm Rd RDV CT15 ....34 D1
Townsend Ter DVW CT17 * 58 B2
Town Wall DVW CT17 * 6 F5
Townwall St DVE/WH CT16 ....5 F5
The Tram Rd FOLKN CT19 ....6 E4
Travers Rd DEAL CT14 ....30 B4
Trenchard Cl KEN/WIL TN24 ....30 B4
Trimworth Rd FOLKN CT19 ....67 F1
Trinity Gdns FOLK CT20 ....6 C6

Trinity Homes DEAL CT14 * 11
Trinity Pl DEAL CT14 6
Trinity St FOLK CT20 6
    KEN/WIL TN24 18
Tritton Cl KEN/WIL TN24 19
Tritton Flds KEN/WIL TN24 19
Troubridge Cl KEN/WIL TN24 30
Tudor Byway KEN/WIL TN24 19
Tudor Ent Rd DEAL CT14 19
Tudor Farm Cl ASH TN23 43
Tudor Rd FOLKN CT19 66
    KEN/WIL TN24 30
Tufton Rd KEN/WIL TN24 3
Tufton St ASH TN23 3
Turketel Rd FOLK CT20 67
Turnbridge Wy ASH TN23 28
Turner Cl KEN/WIL TN24 30
Turners Av TENT TN30 70
Turnpike Cl HYTHE CT21 64
Turnpike Hl HYTHE CT21 64
Tweed Ter HYTHE CT21 * 75
Twelve Acres KEN/WIL TN24 30
Twiss Av HYTHE CT21 65
Twiss Gv HYTHE CT21 65
Twiss Rd HYTHE CT21 65
Tyson Rd FOLKN CT19 54

U

Ulley Rd KEN/WIL TN24 19
Undercliff FOLK CT20 67
Undercliffe Rd DEAL CT14 13
Underdown Rd DVW CT17 4
Underhill Rd FOLK CT20 66
Underwood RFOLK CT18 35
Underwood Cl KEN/WIL TN24 18
Union Quay DVW CT17 4
Union Rd DEAL CT14 9
Union St DVW CT17 4
Uphill FOLK CT20 35
Upper Bridge St RASHE TN25 15
Upper Malthouse Hl HYTHE CT21 64
Upper Rd DVE/WH CT16 13
Upper St DEAL CT14 13
Upper Vicarage Rd
    KEN/WIL TN24 19
Upton Cl FOLKN CT19 53

V

Valebrook Cl FOLK CT20 66
Valestone Cl HYTHE CT21 66
Vale View Rd DVW CT17 3
Valley Rd DVW CT17 3
    FOLK CT20 67
Valley Wk HYTHE CT21 66
Varne Pl FOLKN CT19 7
Varne Rd FOLKN CT19 7
Vernon Pl DEAL CT14 9
Viaduct Ter RASHW TN26 * 72
The Viaduct DVW CT17 58
Viburnum Cl ASH TN23 43
Vicarage La ASH TN23 3
    DEAL CT14 8
    RCANTW CT4 27
    RDV CT15 7
Vickers Cl RFOLK CT18 3
Victoria Av HYTHE CT21 2
Victoria Crs ASH TN23 7
    DVE/WH CT16 31
Victoria Gv FOLK CT20 58
    HYTHE CT21 2
Victoria Ms DEAL CT14 * 11
Victoria Pk DEAL CT14 9
    DVE/WH CT16 5
Victoria Pl HYTHE CT21 * 38
Victoria Rd ASH TN23 28
    DEAL CT14 9
    FOLKN CT19 67
    HYTHE CT21 2
    RFOLK CT18 33
Victoria St DVW CT17 4
Victory Rd RDV CT15 25
Village Wy RASHW TN26 17
Vincent Cl DEAL CT14 9
Viney's Gdns TENT TN30 70
Vlissingen Dr DEAL CT14 30

W

Waddington Dr RFOLK CT18 34
Wainwright Pl KEN/WIL TN24 19
Wakefield Wy HYTHE CT21 64
Walcheren Cl DEAL CT14 11
Wallace Ms FOLKN CT19 54
Wallis Rd KEN/WIL TN24 19
Wall Rd KEN/WIL TN24 19
Walmer Castle Rd DEAL CT14 11
Walmer Cl DEAL CT14 * 11
Walmer Gdns DEAL CT14 11
Walmer Wy DEAL CT14 11
The Waltons FOLKN CT19 54
Walnut Cl KEN/WIL TN24 19
Walnut Tree Ms HYTHE CT21 * 64
Waltham Cl KEN/WIL TN24 19
Walton Gdns FOLKN CT19 54
Walton Manor Cl FOLKN CT19 54
Walton Rd FOLKN CT19 54
The Waltons FOLKN CT19 54
Warden House Ms DEAL CT14 9
Warehorne Rd RASHW TN26 60
Warren Cl FOLKN CT19 3
Warren Hts RASHE TN25 3
Warren La KEN/WIL TN24 30
Warren Rd DEAL CT14 9
The Warren RASHE TN25 3
Warren Vw RASHE TN25 3

Wy FOLKN CT19 ....7 K2
Rd DEAL CT14 ....11 H1
WIL TN24 ....19 G3
rd Farm Rd ASH TN23 ....42 C2
gton Cl DVE/WH CT16 ....38 B1
ook Av KEN/WIL TN24 ....44 B2
ess La ASH TN23 ....2 A7
d Rd RASHW TN26 ....17 E3
arm RCANTW CT4 ....27 H2
o Crs DVW CT17 ....4 E7
d Rd FOLK CT20 ....66 D2
ind DVE/WH CT16 ....21 E4
e KEN/WIL TN24 ....30 B4
t DEAL CT14 ....9 H2
Rd FOLKN CT19 ....6 D1
s Cl RASHE TN25 ....19 E1
Ter TENT TN30 ....70 C2
e Av TENT TN30 ....70 C1
Av TENT TN30 ....70 C2
ald KEN/WIL TN24 ....3 G1
ay Crs FOLKN CT19 ....7 K3
ay Rd FOLKN CT19 ....7 J2
ay Rd DVE/WH CT16 ....4 A1
s Wy ASH TN23 ....28 C5
FOLKN CT19 ....53 H2
- Wy RFOLK CT18 ....35 E4
ay Av DEAL CT14 ....11 G2
y Rd DVE/WH CT16 ....5 F5
y Vls KEN/WIL TN24 * 3 H2
Rd FOLK CT20 ....67 G2
on Ms HYTHE CT21 * 66 A5
on Pde DEAL CT14 ....11 H5
on Pl FOLK CT20 ....66 D4
on Rd DEAL CT14 ....11 H4
WH CT16 ....21 F4
CT20 ....66 D2
on Ter DEAL CT20 * 66 D4
RDV CT15 ....33 E3
FOLK CT18 ....33 E3
TENT TN30 ....70 B4
i FOLKN CT19 ....67 E1
Rd FOLK CT20 ....66 D3
orth Cl RFOLK CT18 ....33 E3
School Rd ASH TN23 ....28 B5
FOLK CT18 ....33 E2
urne ASH TN23 ....42 B1
urne Gdns FOLK CT20 * 6 A6
ry Rd DVW CT17 ....58 D1
ff Gdns FOLK CT20 ....7 F5
oss TENT TN30 ....70 A5
oss Gdns TENT TN30 ....70 A5

West Cross Ms TENT TN30 * 70 A5
Westdean Cl DVW CT17 ....37 G2
Westerhout Cl DEAL CT14 ....9 F1
Western Av ASH TN23 ....2 D3
Western Cl DVW CT17 ....58 C1
Western Gdns KEN/WIL TN24 .....30 A4
Western Rd DEAL CT14 ....9 G5
Westfield La RFOLK CT18 ....51 F1
Westland Wy RFOLK CT18 ....53 H1
West Lawn Gdns FOLK CT20 ......66 D4
West Lea DEAL CT14 ....9 G2
Westmoors ASH TN23 ....42 B1
West Norman Rd DVE/WH CT16 ...4 E4
West Pde HYTHE CT21 ....75 F2
West Rp DVE/WH CT16 ....5 K3
West Rd FOLK CT20 ....66 C3
West Roman Ditch DVE/WH CT16 ...5 E4
West St ASH TN23 ....3 E4
  DEAL CT14 ....9 G2
  DVW CT17 ....4 B3
  HDCN TN27 ....16 A1
West Ter FOLK CT20 ....7 F5
Westwell Ct TENT TN30 * 7 F5
Westwell La RASHW TN26 ....18 A3
Weymouth Cl FOLKN CT19 ....66 D1
Weymouth Rd DEAL CT14 ....66 D1
Weymouth Ter FOLKN CT19 * 52 D5
Wharton Gdns KEN/WIL TN24 .....30 B4
Whinless Rd DVW CT17 ....37 H4
Whiston Av RASHW TN26 ....40 B5
Whitby Rd DEAL CT14 ....66 D1
Whitby Ter DVE/WH CT16 * 38 B1
White Acre Dr DEAL CT14 ....9 H5
Whitebeam Cl ASH TN23 ....17 H5
Whitecliff Wy FOLKN CT19 ....68 D1
White Cl DVW CT17 ....22 B4
Whitehall Wy RASHE TN25 ....4 A5
White Horse Hi RFOLK CT18 ....4 A1
White Horse La RCANTW CT4 ......26 C3
Whitenbrook HYTHE CT21 ....66 A4
White Willow Cl KEN/WIL TN24 ...43 H1
Whitfield Rd ASH TN23 ....91 F4
Whitfield Av DVE/WH CT16 ....38 B2
Whitfield Ct DVE/WH CT16 ....22 B3
Whitfield Hl DVE/WH CT16 ....21 H5
Wickenden Crs KEN/WIL TN24 ....30 C4
The Wickets KEN/WIL TN24 * 30 B5
Widgeon Wk RFOLK CT18 ....53 H1
Widred Rd DVW CT17 ....37 G3
Wilberforce Rd FOLK CT20 ....67 E4
Wilkinson Dr DEAL CT14 ....11 H1
Willesborough Ct KEN/WIL TN24 ...30 C3

Willesborough Rd KEN/WIL TN24 ...30 B1
William Av DVW CT17 ....53 H5
William Judge Cl TENT TN30 ....71 E5
William Pitt Av DEAL CT14 ....9 F5
William Pitt Cl HYTHE CT21 ....65 F5
William Rd ASH TN23 ....29 F4
Willingdon Av DEAL CT14 ....11 G2
Willingdon Pl DEAL CT14 ....11 G2
Willow Cl DVE/WH CT16 ....22 A4
Willow Cl HYTHE CT21 ....74 C1
Willow Dr RASHW TN26 ....72 B4
Willow Rd DEAL CT14 ....10 A1
The Willows KEN/WIL TN24 ....19 F3
  RASHW TN26 ....30 B3
Willow Tree La KEN/WIL TN24 ......30 B3
Wilson Av DEAL CT14 ....10 D1
Wilson Cl KEN/WIL TN24 ....30 D3
Wiltie Gdns FOLKN CT19 ....6 D3
Wilton Cl DEAL CT14 ....9 F4
Wilton Rd FOLKN CT19 ....6 A2
Winant Wy DVE/WH CT16 ....38 B1
Winchelsea Cl DVW CT17 ....4 A5
Winchelsea Rd DVW CT17 ....4 A5
Winchelsea Ter DVW CT17 ....4 A5
Winchester Ms DEAL CT14 ....11 F1
Windmill Cl KEN/WIL TN24 ....75 C1
Windmill St HYTHE CT21 ....75 F1
Winehouse La RFOLK CT18 ....55 C1
Wingate Rd FOLKN CT19 ....54 B5
Wingrove Hl DVW CT17 ....37 G2
Winnipeg Cl DVE/WH CT16 ....38 B1
Winterage La RFOLK CT18 ....34 A2
Winter Dr RFOLK CT18 ....35 E4
Wissenden La RASHW TN26 ....40 B2
Wivenhoe ASH TN23 ....42 C2
Wolfe Ter DVE/WH CT16 * 38 B1
Wollaston Rd DEAL CT14 ....9 H5
Wolseley Pl KEN/WIL TN24 * 5 F2
Wood Av FOLKN CT19 ....54 B5
Woodbury La TENT TN30 ....70 B5
Woodchurch Rd RASHW TN26 ....5 K4
  TENT TN30 ....70 D4
Woodcock Gdns RFOLK CT18 ......34 C5
Wood Cottage La FOLKN CT19 ....52 D5
Woodfield Av RFOLK CT18 ....53 E5
Woodfield Cl FOLKN CT19 ....52 D5
Woodland Cl DVW CT17 ....37 G2
Woodland Rd RFOLK CT18 ....52 D5
Woodlands ASH TN23 * 4 A3
Woodlands Dr HYTHE CT21 ....66 A3
Woodlands Rd KEN/WIL TN24 .....30 B2
Wood La ASH TN23 ....43 G4

Woodlea KEN/WIL TN24 ....3 H1
Wood Rd HYTHE CT21 ....64 D5
Woodside ASH TN23 ....42 B1
Woodside Cl DVE/WH CT16 ....21 G5
Wood's Pl DVW CT17 ....38 B2
Woodstock Rd DEAL CT14 ....9 G5
Woodstock Wy KEN/WIL TN24 ....19 E5
The Woodyard DEAL CT14 * 9 H3
Woolcomber St DVW CT17 ....5 G5
Woolmer Dr KEN/WIL TN24 ....30 C5
Woolpack Hl RASHE TN25 ....46 D2
Woolreeds Rd ASH TN23 ....42 B5
Worthington St DVW CT17 ....4 D4
Worth La FOLK CT20 ....67 G4
Wotton Rd ASH TN23 ....43 F1
Wrights Cl TENT TN30 ....70 B4
Wych Elm Wy HYTHE CT21 ....74 C1
Wycherley Crs DVE/WH CT16 ......22 B5
Wyndham Rd DVW CT17 ....4 A4
Wyndham Wy RASHE TN25 ....18 B5
Wyndy La RASHE TN25 ....18 B5
Wyvern Wy KEN/WIL TN24 ....30 A1

Y

Yeoman Gdns KEN/WIL TN24 ......30 C3
Yew Cl ASH TN23 ....28 C2
Yew Tree Cl DEAL CT14 * 9 F5
  RASHE TN25 ....49 F5
Yew Tree Ms DEAL CT14 ....11 E1
York & Albany Cl DEAL CT14 ....11 F3
York Ms FOLKN CT19 * 53 E5
York Rd DEAL CT14 ....11 H1
  KEN/WIL TN24 ....19 F4
York St DVW CT17 ....4 E5
York Street Rbt DVW CT17 ....4 E6
Young Cl DEAL CT14 ....9 F3
Young's Pl RDV CT15 ....56 B2

Z

Zarena Ct FOLK CT20 * 67 F4

dex - featured places

vel Centre
  WH CT16 ....5 K4
s CE Primary School
  CT19 ....67 E1
nford Ten Pin
  ling Centre
  N23 ....3 H4
fe Fort
  CT17 ....58 D2
s Court Maths
  mputing College
  WH CT16 ....22 B4
s Court School
  WH CT16 ....22 B4
d Borough Museum
  N23 ....3 F4
d Business Park
  WIL TN24 ....44 C1
d Civic Centre
  N23 ....3 H4
d College
  N23 ....3 H4
d International Hotel
  WIL TN24 ....18 D5
d (Kent) Golf Club
  WIL TN24 ....18 B2
d Market
  WIL TN24 ....44 B1
d School
  WIL TN24 ....3 H3
d South CP School
  CT17 ....2 C7
d Town FC
  WH CT16 ....61 H2
ollege for the Arts
  CT17 ....4 A4
heatre
  CT14 ....9 G3
e CP School
  CT17 ....58 A3
Junior School
  WH CT16 ....38 C2
y Museum
  CT15 ....25 F5
Industrial Estate
  N23 ....29 F5
n Business Park
  N23 ....62 D1
estern
  chill Hotel
  CT17 ....5 F6
estern Clifton Hotel
  CT20 ....6 C6
sden Primary School
  WH TN26 ....40 C2
Memorial
  WH CT16 ....5 H2
Road Business Centre
  N23 ....2 B3
tish School
  N23 ....9 H2
ill Country Park
  HE CT21 ....64 B3
ill Park School (Lower)
  HE CT21 ....64 C4
ill Park School (Upper)
  HE CT21 ....64 C3
ield Industrial Estate
  N23 ....2 A5

Buckland Cemetery
  DVE/WH CT16 ....38 D2
Buckland Hospital
  DVW CT17 ....38 A3
Capel Le Ferne Primary School
  RFOLK CT18 ....55 G1
Castle Clinic
  CT17 ....5 F4
Castle Community College
  DVW CT17 ....9 G5
The Channel School
  FOLKN CT19 ....54 A1
Channel Tunnel Exhibition
  Centre RFOLK CT18 ....52 B4
Channel Tunnel
  Passenger Terminal
  RFOLK CT18 ....52 B4
Channel Tunnel Rail Link
  KEN/WIL TN24 ....29 H4
  RASHE TN25 ....17 G2
  RASHE TN25 ....45 H5
Charlton CE Primary School
  DVE/WH CT16 ....38 C2
Charlton Shopping Centre
  DVE/WH CT16 ....4 C3
Cheriton Primary School
  FOLK CT20 ....66 C1
Cheriton Road Cemetery
  FOLK CT20 ....67 G2
Christ Church CE Primary School
  FOLK CT20 ....6 D5
Christ Church High School
  ASH TN23 ....42 D2
Chunnel Industrial Estate
  ASH TN23 ....3 F6
The Churchill School
  RFOLK CT18 ....34 D5
Cineworld
  RASHE TN25 ....19 E4
Clarendon & Westbury
  Community Centre
  DVW CT17 ....4 A6
Cobbs Wood Industrial Estate
  ASH TN23 ....2 A3
Coldecott School
  RASHE TN25 ....46 B4
Connaught Barracks (MOD)
  RDV CT15 ....39 E2
County Square Shopping Centre
  ASH TN23 ....3 F3
Cowgate Cemetery
  DVW CT17 ....4 D5
Crabble Corn Mill
  DVW CT17 ....37 H1
Cruise Liner Terminal 1
  DVW CT17 ....59 E2
Cruise Liner Terminal 2
  DVW CT17 ....59 F3
Customs & Excise Offices
  DVW CT17 ....4 B4
Deal Castle
  DEAL CT14 ....9 H4
Deal Cemetery
  DEAL CT14 ....9 F5
The Deal Maritime
  & Local History Museum
  DEAL CT14 ....9 H3
Deal Rowing Club
  DEAL CT14 ....9 H2

Deal Squash & Racket Club
  DEAL CT14 ....9 H1
Deal Town FC
  DEAL CT14 ....9 F5
Deal Victoria & Barnes CC
  DEAL CT14 ....11 F2
Deal & Walmer Community
  Health Clinic
  DEAL CT14 ....9 F4
De Bradelei Wharf Shopping Centre
  DVW CT17 ....4 E6
Dering Wood Nature Reserve
  RASHW TN26 ....16 D1
The Dover Business Centre
  DVW CT17 ....4 B6
Dover Castle
  & Secret Wartime Tunnels
  DVE/WH CT16 ....5 H4
Dover College
  DVW CT17 ....4 C4
Dover Grammar School for Boys
  DVE/WH CT16 ....38 A4
Dover Grammar School for Girls
  DVE/WH CT16 ....4 C1
Dover Harbour Board Offices
  DVW CT17 ....5 F6
Dover Health Centre
  DVW CT17 ....4 E3
Dover Leisure Centre
  DVE/WH CT16 ....5 G4
Dover Museum
  DVW CT17 ....4 E5
Dover Pharos
  DVE/WH CT16 ....5 H3
Dover Water Sports Centre
  DVW CT17 ....5 F6
The Downs CE Primary School
  DEAL CT14 ....11 F2
Downsview Infant School
  KEN/WIL TN24 ....19 G2
The Drop Redoubt
  DVW CT17 ....4 D6
Dunkerleys Hotel & Restaurant
  DEAL CT14 ....9 H3
East Kent Business Centre
  DVW CT17 ....5 F6
Eastmead Trading Estate
  ASH TN23 ....3 G7
East Stour Primary School
  KEN/WIL TN24 ....43 H1
Eden Business Centre
  DVW CT17 ....4 A5
Elham CE Primary School
  RCANTW CT4 ....27 H2
Ellingham Industrial Centre
  ASH TN23 ....43 E2
Enterprise Business Centre
  DVE/WH CT16 ....22 A3
Etchinghill Golf Club
  RFOLK CT18 ....33 F5
Eureka Leisure Park
  RASHE TN25 ....19 E4
The Eurogate Business Park
  ASH TN23 ....3 F3
  KEN/WIL TN24 ....18 D4
Evegate Business Centre
  RASHE TN25 ....46 B5
Fairview Industrial Park
  RASHW TN26 ....73 E4

Fairwood Industrial Park
  ASH TN23 ....2 C4
Flicks Cinema
  DEAL CT14 ....9 H3
Folkestone C & CC Site
  FOLKN CT19 ....55 E5
Folkestone CC
  FOLKN CT19 ....67 G1
Folkestone Invicta FC
  FOLKN CT19 ....67 G1
Folkestone Racecourse
  HYTHE CT21 ....63 G1
Folkestone RFC
  RFOLK CT18 ....65 G1
Folkestone Rowing Club
  FOLK CT20 ....67 F4
The Folkestone School
  for Girls
  FOLKN CT19 ....67 F3
Folkestone Sports Centre
  & Ski Slope
  FOLKN CT19 ....6 B1
Folkestone Warren
  Nature Reserve
  FOLKN CT19 ....55 E5
Folkestone Yacht
  & Motor Boat Club
  FOLKN CT19 ....7 J4
Foxwood Special School
  HYTHE CT21 ....65 H5
Freight Services Centre
  DVE/WH CT16 ....5 K4
Furley Park Primary School
  ASH TN23 ....43 G5
Gateway to the White Cliffs (NT)
  DVE/WH CT16 ....39 G3
George Spurgen Community
  Primary School
  FOLKN CT19 ....54 C5
Godinton House
  ASH TN23 ....17 G5
Godinton Primary School
  ASH TN23 ....28 B1
Godinton Way Industrial Estate
  ASH TN23 ....2 E4
Goldwyn Community
  Special School
  ASH TN23 ....17 F5
Grace Chapel & Christian School
  FOLK CT20 ....7 F4
Grand Shaft (Lower Entrance)
  DVW CT17 ....4 D7
Grand Shaft (Upper Entrance)
  DVW CT17 ....4 C7
Great Chart CC
  ASH TN23 ....28 A3
Great Chart Primary School
  ASH TN23 ....28 B4
Grosvenor CE Primary School
  RDV CT15 ....39 E1
Ham Street Primary School
  RASHW TN26 ....72 A3
Hamstreet Woods National
  Nature Reserve
  RASHW TN26 ....72 C3
Harbour School
  DVW CT17 ....37 G5
Harcourt CP School
  FOLKN CT19 ....53 E5

Harvey Clinic
FOLK CT20 .... 6 D4
The Harvey Grammar School
FOLKN CT19 .... 67 G1
Hawkinge Cemetery
RFOLK CT18 .... 34 C4
Hawkinge Crematorium
RFOLK CT18 .... 34 C4
Hawkinge Health Centre
RFOLK CT18 .... 35 E5
Hawkins Clinic
DEAL CT14 .... 9 G3
Henwood Business Centre
KEN/WIL TN24 .... 3 K3
Henwood Industrial Estate
KEN/WIL TN24 .... 3 K2
Highfield Industrial Estate
FOLKN CT19 .... 7 J1
Highworth Grammar School
for Girls
KEN/WIL TN24 .... 2 D1
Hillside Industrial Estate
FOLK CT20 .... 67 E3
Hilton Business Centre
ASH TN23 .... 43 F1
HM Young Offender Institution
DVW CT17 .... 58 B1
Homewood School
TENT TN30 .... 70 C3
Hopewell School
ASH TN23 .... 28 C5
Hothfield Village
Primary School
RASHW TN26 .... 16 D2
Hull Park Sports Club
DEAL CT14 .... 8 D3
Hythe Community Clinic
HYTHE CT21 .... 65 E5
Hythe Community School
HYTHE CT21 .... 75 F1
Hythe CC
HYTHE CT21 .... 65 E5
Hythe Imperial Golf Club
HYTHE CT21 .... 65 G5
The Hythe Imperial Hotel
HYTHE CT21 .... 75 H1
Hythe Ranges
HYTHE CT21 .... 74 C3
Hythe St Leonard CE
Junior School
HYTHE CT21 .... 64 D5
Hythe & Saltwood Sailing Club
HYTHE CT21 .... 75 G1
Hythe Swimming Pool
HYTHE CT21 .... 75 H1
Imperial College London
RASHE TN25 .... 15 E2
The Julie Rose Stadium
KEN/WIL TN24 .... 19 H5
Kearsney Abbey
DVE/WH CT16 .... 21 F5
Keith Graham Academy
FOLK CT20 .... 7 G4
Kengate Industrial Estate
HYTHE CT21 .... 74 D1
Kennington CE Junior School
KEN/WIL TN24 .... 19 F2
Kennington CC
KEN/WIL TN24 .... 19 F2
Kent Battle of Britain Museum
RFOLK CT18 .... 53 F1
Kingsdown & Ringwould CE
Primary School
DEAL CT14 .... 13 G2
Kings North CE Primary School
ASH TN23 .... 43 F4
Kingsnorth Industrial Estate
ASH TN23 .... 43 F1
Knights Templar Church (Ruins)
DVW CT17 .... 58 C1
Lady Joanna Thornhill
(Endowed) Primary School
RASHE TN25 .... 15 E2
Linden Grove Primary School
ASH TN23 .... 43 E1
Little Satmar Holiday Park
RFOLK CT18 .... 55 G1
Little Switzerland Camping
& Caravan Site
RFOLK CT18 .... 55 E4
Little Theatre
FOLK CT20 .... 67 E4
Longport Police Station
RFOLK CT18 .... 52 B5
Lydden CP School
RDV CT15 .... 20 B1
Lyminge CE Primary School
RFOLK CT18 .... 33 E2
Lympne CE Primary School
HYTHE CT21 .... 63 E4
Lympne Industrial Estate
HYTHE CT21 .... 62 C4

Mace Industrial Estate
KEN/WIL TN24 .... 3 H2
Maison Dieu House
DVE/WH CT16 .... 4 D3
Manor Clinic
FOLK CT20 .... 6 D5
Marina Office
DVW CT17 .... 58 D1
Marine Road Clinic
DEAL CT14 .... 9 H4
Marlborough Road
Industrial Estate
DEAL CT14 .... 10 D2
Martello Industrial Estate
FOLKN CT19 .... 7 K1
McArthur Glen
Designer Outlet
KEN/WIL TN24 .... 29 G5
Meadow View
Industrial Estate
RASHW TN26 .... 72 D4
Melbourne CP School
DVE/WH CT16 .... 22 C5
Mersham Primary School
RASHE TN25 .... 45 G4
The Mildmay Hotel
DVW CT17 .... 4 B5
Minters Industrial Estate
DEAL CT14 .... 8 C5
Mongeham Primary School
DEAL CT14 .... 8 D5
Montpelier Business Park
ASH TN23 .... 2 B5
Morehall Primary School
FOLKN CT19 .... 67 F1
Mundella Primary School
FOLKN CT19 .... 6 E1
The North School
KEN/WIL TN24 .... 3 K5
The Norton Knatchbull School
ASH TN23 .... 30 A2
Oak Tree CP School
ASH TN23 .... 2 B7
Old Ashford Cemetery
KEN/WIL TN24 .... 3 G1
Old Hospital
RCANTW CT4 .... 27 H1
Old Railway Works
(Industrial Estate)
KEN/WIL TN24 .... 29 H4
Old St James' Church (ruins)
KEN/WIL TN24 .... 5 G4
Orbital Park
KEN/WIL TN24 .... 44 B1
Palmarsh Primary School
HYTHE CT21 .... 74 B2
Park Farm Industrial Estate
FOLKN CT19 .... 53 H4
Park Farm Primary School
FOLKN CT19 .... 54 A5
Park Farm Recreation Centre
ASH TN23 .... 43 E3
Park Farm Retail Park
FOLKN CT19 .... 53 H4
Park Mall Shopping Centre
KEN/WIL TN24 .... 3 F3
Pencester Surgery
DVE/WH CT16 .... 4 E4
Pennypot Industrial Estate
HYTHE CT21 .... 74 D1
Pent Valley Technology College
FOLKN CT19 .... 53 F5
Phoenix Community
Primary School
KEN/WIL TN24 .... 19 F4
The Pines Garden
RDV CT15 .... 25 E5
Portal House School
RDV CT15 .... 25 E4
Port Lympne Wild Animal Park,
Mansion & Garden
HYTHE CT21 .... 62 A5
P&O Stena Line
DVW CT17 .... 58 C2
Poulton Business Park
DVW CT17 .... 37 H3
The Powell Schooll
DVE/WH CT16 .... 22 B5
Premier Inn
DVE/WH CT16 .... 5 G5
FOLKN CT19 .... 53 G5
KEN/WIL TN24 .... 44 B2
DVE/WH CT16 .... 23 F5
DVE/WH CT16 .... 57 E3
Prince of Wales Pier
DVW CT17 .... 59 E1
Priory Fields School
DVW CT17 .... 4 A4
Quality Hotel
FOLK CT20 .... 6 B7
Ramada Hotel
DVE/WH CT16 .... 21 H3

Range Road Industrial Estate
HYTHE CT21 .... 75 E1
The Ripple School
DEAL CT14 .... 10 A4
Ripplevale School
DEAL CT14 .... 10 C4
River CP School
DVW CT17 .... 37 G1
Riverside Business Park
KEN/WIL TN24 .... 3 J3
Riverside School
ASH TN23 .... 2 A5
The River Surgery
DVW CT17 .... 21 G5
Roman Painted House
DVE/WH CT16 .... 4 E5
Romney Hythe & Dymchurch
Railway
HYTHE CT21 .... 74 D1
Royal Cinque Ports Yacht Club
DVE/WH CT16 .... 5 F6
Royal Victoria Hospital
FOLKN CT19 .... 6 C2
St Eanswythes CE Primary School
FOLK CT20 .... 7 G5
St Edmunds Catholic School
DVE/WH CT16 .... 38 C2
St George's Business Centre
ASH TN23 .... 28 C2
St Margarets at Cliffe
Primary School
RDV CT15 .... 25 E4
St Martins CE Primary School
FOLK CT20 .... 66 B2
St Martins School
DVE/WH CT16 .... 38 A5
St Mary CE Primary School
FOLKN CT19 .... 7 K1
St Marys CE Primary School
ASH TN23 .... 2 D2
St Marys RC Primary School
DEAL CT14 .... 5 F3
St Marys RC Primary School
DEAL CT14 .... 10 D1
St Marys Westbrook
FOLKN CT19 .... 67 G2
St Michaels CE Primary School
TENT TN30 .... 70 C1
St Peters CE Primary School
FOLKN CT19 .... 7 J4
St Radigund's Abbey
RDV CT15 .... 36 D4
St Radigunds Community
Primary School
DVW CT17 .... 38 A3
St Richards RC Primary School
DVE/WH CT16 .... 4 C1
St Simon of England RC
Primary School
ASH TN23 .... 29 E4
St Teresas RC Primary School
KEN/WIL TN24 .... 18 C5
Saltwood CE Primary School
HYTHE CT21 .... 64 D3
Samphire Hoe Country Park
RDV CT15 .... 57 F4
Sandgate Primary School
FOLK CT20 .... 67 F3
Sandown Clinic
DEAL CT14 .... 9 H1
Sandown Primary School
DEAL CT14 .... 9 G2
Seabrook CE Primary School
HYTHE CT21 .... 66 B5
Sellindge Primary School
RASHE TN25 .... 48 A3
Sellindge Sports Club
RASHE TN25 .... 48 B3
Sene Valley Golf Club
RFOLK CT18 .... 65 G3
Shatterlocks Infant School
DVE/WH CT16 .... 38 B2
Shearway Business Park
FOLKN CT19 .... 53 F4
Shell & Dunkirk Memorials
DVW CT17 .... 5 F6
Shepway Cross
HYTHE CT21 .... 63 E5
Sholden CE Primary School
DEAL CT14 .... 8 C4
Shorncliffe Military Cemetery
FOLK CT20 .... 66 C4
Shorncliffe Industrial Estate
FOLK CT20 .... 66 D3
Sibton Park School
RFOLK CT18 .... 32 D1
Silver Screen Cinema
DVE/WH CT16 .... 5 F4
DVE/WH CT16 .... 7 F5
Singleton Medical Centre
ASH TN23 .... 28 B4
Smeeth CP School
RASHE TN25 .... 46 D2

The Southcliff Hotel
FOLK CT20 ....
South Kent College
ASH TN23 ....
ASH TN23 ....
DVE/WH CT16 ....
FOLK CT20 ....
FOLK CT20 ....
South Kent Hospital
FOLK CT20 ....
Southwall Industrial Estate
DEAL CT14 ....
Spring Grove School
RASHE TN25 ....
Stade Court Hotel
HYTHE CT21 ....
Stanhope CP School
ASH TN23 ....
Stella Maris Catholic
Primary School
FOLKN CT19 ....
Stour Leisure Centre
ASH TN23 ....
TA Centre
ASH TN23 ....
Technical Procurement
Sports Club
RASHE TN25 ....
Temple Ewell CE
Primary School
DVE/WH CT16 ....
Tenterden CE Junior School
TENT TN30 ....
Tenterden Golf Club
TENT TN30 ....
Tenterden Infant School
TENT TN30 ....
Tenterden Leisure Centre
TENT TN30 ....
The Towers School
KEN/WIL TN24 ....
Travelodge
RASHE TN25 ....
Vale View Community School
DVW CT17 ....
Victoria Hospital
DEAL CT14 ....
Victoria Road Primary School
ASH TN23 ....
Wallett's Court
Country House Hotel
RDV CT15 ....
Walmer Castle & Gardens
DEAL CT14 ....
Walmer & Kingsdown Golf Club
DEAL CT14 ....
Walmer Lawn Tennis
& Croquet Club
DEAL CT14 ....
Warden House Primary School
DEAL CT14 ....
Warren Retail Park
DEAL CT14 ....
Westmount Centre
DVW CT17 ....
White Cliffs Business Park
DVW CT17 ....
White Cliffs Experience
DVW CT17 ....
Whitehouse Surgery
DVW CT17 ....
Whitfield & Aspen
Primary School
DVE/WH CT16 ....
Whitfield Surgery
DVE/WH CT16 ....
Willesborough Cemetery
KEN/WIL TN24 ....
Willesborough Health Centre
KEN/WIL TN24 ....
Willesborough Industrial Park
KEN/WIL TN24 ....
Willesborough Primary School
KEN/WIL TN24 ....
William Harvey Hospital
KEN/WIL TN24 ....
The Woodland Garden Cemetery
RASHE TN25 ....
Wotton Trading Estate
ASH TN23 ....
Wye Business Park
RASHE TN25 ....
The Wyvern School
KEN/WIL TN24 ....

Acknowledgements

Schools address data provided by Education Direct.

Petrol station information supplied by Johnsons.

Garden centre information provided by:

Garden Centre Association  Britains best garden centres

Wyevale Garden Centres

The statement on the front cover of this atlas is sourced, selected and quoted
from a reader comment and feedback form received in 2004